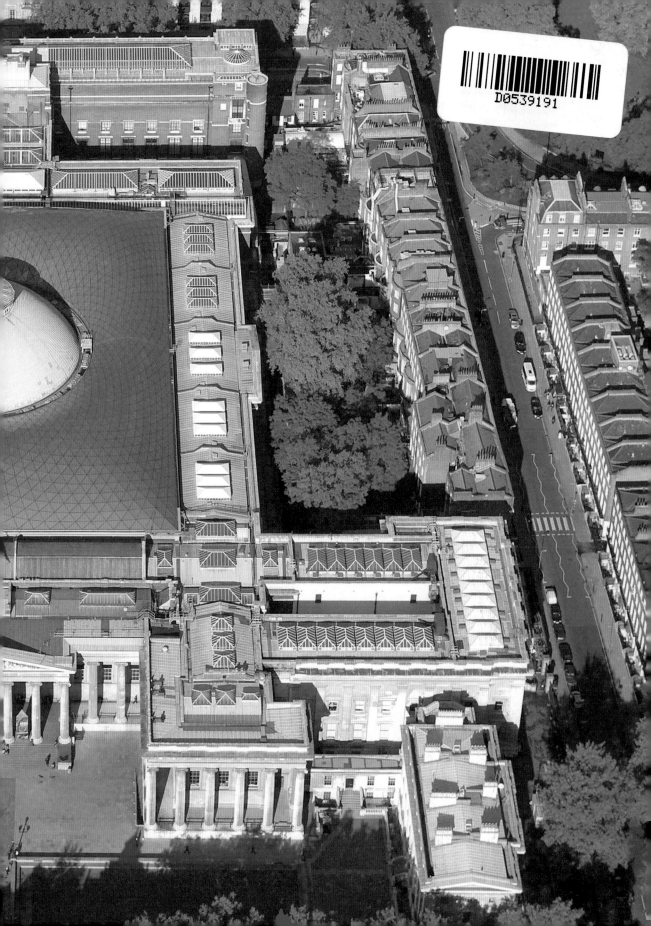

THE MUSEUM

THE MUSEUM

Behind the scenes at the British Museum

RUPERT SMITH

BBC
BOOKS

This book is published to accompany the television series entitled *The Museum*, first broadcast on BBC2 in 2007.

10 9 8 7 6 5 4 3 2

Published in 2007 by BBC Books, an imprint of Ebury Publishing.
Ebury Publishing is a division of the Random House Group.

The Random House Group Limited Reg. No. 954009

Addresses for companies within the Random House Group can be found at
www.randomhouse.co.uk

A CIP catalogue record for this book is available from the British Library.

ISBN 978 0 563 53913 1

The Random House Group Limited makes every effort to ensure that the papers
used in our books are made from trees that have been legally sourced from
well-managed and credibly certified forests. Our paper procurement policy can
be found at www.randomhouse.co.uk

Commissioning editor: Martin Redfern
Project editor: Christopher Tinker
Copy editor: Helen Armitage
Designer: Linda Blakemore
Production controller: David Brimble

Colour origination and printing by Butler & Tanner Ltd, Frome, England

*The author and BBC Books would like to thank the staff of the British Museum
for their invaluable help in putting together this book.*

Contents

The British Museum exists to tell the story of mankind. It is where our history can be traced from the earliest artefacts made in Africa nearly 2 million years ago to the most contemporary work produced around the globe; where the world's cultural heritage has been collected, conserved, investigated and debated since the Museum was founded by Parliament in 1753; and where an increasing number and variety of people have come to visit ever since.

Today the British Museum is no longer just a building in Bloomsbury. It has both a real and a virtual presence the world over, reaching a new international audience that stretches from Bristol to Beijing, from Newcastle to Nairobi, from Wrexham to Ramallah. The purpose of communicating with this global community is to provide access to our collections, of course. But through and beyond this is the desire to foster dialogue, collaboration and understanding of the world's cultural interconnectedness.

This world community consists of any number of local communities, starting with the body of people who comprise the trustees, staff and volunteers of the British Museum itself. They come from many different backgrounds and places of origin, bringing a wealth of experience – personal, cultural and linguistic – to place at the service of our many different audiences. Their commitment to the care of the collection and to putting it to work for public benefit results in a vitality that speaks through the voices and activities contained within this book.

Parliament's purpose in establishing the Museum in 1753 was to facilitate public understanding of the complexity and unity of human cultural achievements. Vital to this endeavour are not only the scholarship of the Museum's expert staff, but what the Museum's visitors and users the world over can contribute. For it is above all through their constant re-engagement with the Museum that new meanings and understandings are generated, and the collection is made new for each successive generation.

Neil MacGregor, Director of the British Museum

1

'For the use and benefit of the publick'

The British Museum was founded in 1753 with a simple mission statement: to preserve its collection 'for the use and benefit of the publick, who may have free access to view and peruse the same'. Not only that – it aimed also to present a universal collection, drawing on all categories of human history, culture and knowledge.

It sounds obvious enough, but those basic founding principles of universality and free access made the British Museum unique in its time and now, half way through its third century, one of the most famous and revered institutions in the world. Various pressures – of funding, maintenance, ethics, politics, war – have shaped the direction that the Museum has taken over the years, but it remains true to those 'fundamental principles from which the Trustees do not think they can in Honor or conscience depart'. Principles forged in the intellectual heat of the Enlightenment are just as challenging in the twenty-first century, and, while the details change, the underlying ideas remain as solid as marble.

The collection has its roots in the intellectual curiosity of one man, Sir Hans Sloane, an Irish doctor who began collecting during a posting to Jamaica as the governor's personal physician. Returning to London in 1687, he built up a successful and extremely lucrative medical practice – his patients included the diarist Samuel Pepys and Queen Anne – and poured his excess income into his collection. Before long, his house in Bloomsbury Place was crammed full of 'plants, fossils, minerals, zoological, anatomical and pathological specimens, antiquities … prints, drawings and coins, books and manuscripts'. The collection overflowed its premises, so Sloane was obliged to buy the house next door as well – and when that was full, he moved lock, stock and barrel to a manor house in Chelsea. Visitors flocked to view Sloane's curiosities, and long before his death in 1753 the collection had become one of the must-see attractions of London.

Although the marvellous and the bizarre were to be found among Sloane's collection, such as a landscape painted on a spider's web or monstrous stones taken from the bladders of horses, he planned his acquisitions with care, especially with regard to natural history. He was conscious of collecting not just for himself, but for the scholarly world at large as well, working through a network of contacts who sent him material from far and wide. When Sloane died, an Act of Parliament was passed to acquire his

Below: Sir Hans Sloane (1660–1753), physician and collector, whose bequest of books, manuscripts, pictures, coins and curiosities formed the basis of the British Museum.

Opposite: The Queen Elizabeth II Great Court, the largest covered square in Europe. Its tessellated glass roof was designed by Foster & Partners.

collection of 80,000 objects for the sum of £20,000, according to the terms of his will, and vest it in a board of trustees who would be responsible for maintaining the collection 'intire without the least diminution or separation' and making it publicly accessible. The British Museum Act 1753 laid down those guiding principles, which, with minor alterations, continue to govern the management of the collection.

The trustees' first task was to find a home not just for the Sloane collection but also for a priceless collection of manuscripts that had been established as a public collection by Parliament in 1700. The Cottonian Library, assembled by the family of Sir Robert Bruce Cotton, included the Lindisfarne Gospels, a manuscript of Beowulf and two copies of Magna Carta. But, despite its inestimable value, the collection had languished in damp and decaying houses for 50 years and narrowly escaped being entirely destroyed by fire. The government, seeing an opportunity to take care of an embarrassing legacy, added the Cottonian Library and some other, smaller collections to the British Museum's charge.

Potential premises in the Palace of Westminster and Buckingham House (now Buckingham Palace) were rejected as too costly, and the trustees finally bought Montagu House, a seventeenth-century mansion in Bloomsbury with seven and a half acres of grounds, for £10,000. After an extensive programme of renovations, the new museum opened for business in 1759 – and it has remained open on the same spot ever since. Nothing remains of the original Montagu House, gradually demolished and replaced in a series of additions and rebuildings in the nineteenth century, but the front railings on Great Russell Street mark the site of its old outer wall.

No sooner was the British Museum established than it started to attract more objects for the collection. The first Egyptian mummy was bequeathed in 1756, and the following year the king (George II) donated the old Royal Library, a collection of 12,000 books dating back to the fifteenth century. From 1800, the great and the good were falling over themselves to give or sell their collections to the nation. The Museum's reputation was sealed in 1802 by the arrival of a 'pierre de granite noir chargée de trois bandes de charactères' – the Rosetta stone – discovered by Napoleon's troops in Egypt and surrendered to the British under the Treaty of Alexandria. The stone became an instant focus of interest, both public and academic, and remains a BM icon.

The Rosetta stone … became an instant focus of interest … and remains a BM icon

As the collections grew, and with them public interest, it became clear that

Left: Montagu House, first home of the collection.
Below: The construction of the Reading Room, which was completed in 1857.

Montagu House was no longer big enough for the job. It had already cost tens of thousands of pounds to renovate and could no longer sustain the number of objects or the rate of footfall required of it, so the trustees appointed architect Sir Robert Smirke to oversee the gradual demolition of the old building and the creation of new, purpose-built museum premises. His plans were approved in 1827, and substantial building works continued until 1857 when the completion of the Reading Room gave us, essentially, the core of the Museum building that we know today.

Changes continued throughout the nineteenth century as more collections arrived in Bloomsbury, but despite the constant enlargement of the building, something had to give. The first major demarcation of the collections came with the departure of the botanical and zoological objects to the newly established Natural History Museum, which opened in 1881, leaving space for the display of larger items, such as the Mausoleum at Halikarnassus. Further space was acquired by the purchase of 69 houses surrounding the Museum in 1895, turning it into something resembling a small town within a town, bordered by Great Russell Street, Bloomsbury Street, Montague Place and Montague Street.

And so the British Museum entered the twentieth century, surviving two world wars, despite a number of direct hits during the Blitz of 1940, continually

Above: The Museum's team of specialist cleaners set about cleaning the 1656 pairs of glass panes that make up the roof of the Great Court.

expanding its collections and widening the scope of its academic ambition. The last great split came in 1972 with the British Library Act, which established the British Library as a separate institutional entity partially sharing its premises with the Museum. After a long planning period, a purpose-built library on London's Euston Road opened in 1998, not only leaving room in the Museum for extra gallery space where books were once stored, but also paving the way for the development of the Great Court. This final, iconic addition to the Museum, with its billowing Norman Foster roof, was opened in 2000, ushering in a new era of public access and confirming the British Museum's status as one of the world's most important cultural institutions.

Throughout two and a half centuries of change and growth, the British Museum has remained close to its eighteenth-century intellectual roots. 'The idea of universal access to an encyclopedic collection is there in the

founding act,' says BM director Neil MacGregor. 'We maintain a collection of things from the whole world that will be freely accessible to the people of the whole world. We try to reinterpret those principles for each new generation, but however much the details change, we remain true to the basic Enlightenment ideals. Funnily enough, the newspapers tend to refer to the concept of universal access as being "politically correct" – but if that is the case, it's been politically correct for over 250 years.'

The British Museum collection is unique in being housed entirely under one roof. The building in Bloomsbury is an important London landmark, celebrated in popular song, a magnet for tourists and a resource for local people. 'It's always been one of the great sights of London,' says MacGregor. 'Ever since the late eighteenth century, tourists have been coming

... a collection from the whole world ... freely accessible to the people of the whole world

**NEIL
MACGREGOR**

Director of the
British Museum

I CAME HERE FROM THE NATIONAL GALLERY, where I was director until 2002. I knew that my predecessor, Robert Anderson, was retiring, and this seemed to me to be by far the most challenging museum job in the world – for the simple reason that there is no other museum like it in the world. If you're interested in public engagement with cultural history, this is the place to be.

The scale and diversity of the collection is the most striking thing about the British Museum. Whereas at the National Gallery you're dealing with the paintings of Europe, here you're dealing with the cultures of the world. The National Gallery is one type of object – paintings on canvas – and one discipline, art history. The British Museum has all kinds of objects and therefore needs much wider skills: archaeology, art history, connoisseurship, anthropology, science, conservation, cataloguing; the list goes on. It's a bit like being the head of a university, rather than the head of just one department. My job is to balance resources and engagement across a range of very disparate areas, in most of which I have no knowledge, let alone expertise. But the director has to have a view and has to inform himself about the background to the issues – so I listen to a lot of colleagues and do a great deal of reading!

I arrived at the Museum at a time of considerable financial crisis, when the funding was absolutely static, but the costs had risen, and it was quite clear that we couldn't go on as we were. The first thing to do was to stabilize the finance, and that meant, unfortunately, losing a lot of staff. I had to reduce the staff by 10 per cent, which was a brutal thing to do, especially to people who had been here all their working lives. But everyone knew that the financial position was very bad and that redundancies were inevitable. The experience was traumatic for the staff, but we are now able to focus on building a better future.

This is by far the most demanding job I've ever had, in terms of time and everything else. I used to write a lot when I was at the National Gallery and make television programmes, but there's very little opportunity for that sort of thing now. My working day is organized around a series of set meetings with colleagues, but after that it's entirely demand-led. A good deal of the job is representational – we receive important visitors from the UK and abroad, government officials or heads of state. It could be the Prime Minister of Mongolia or the Queen of Denmark and so on. There's a good deal of travel too: about a fifth of my year is taken up with travel, which gives me a lot of time to do all that reading. One of the best things about the job is visiting other collections around the UK, but I also make a lot of long-haul journeys all over the world; to places such as Cairo, Beijing, Nairobi and Tehran.

The job of the director is to address the balance of the safety of the collection, research on the collection and public benefit. Those three things are often in conflict. For instance, we'd like to have part of the drawings collection permanently on show or permanently travelling, but that would destroy it for future generations.

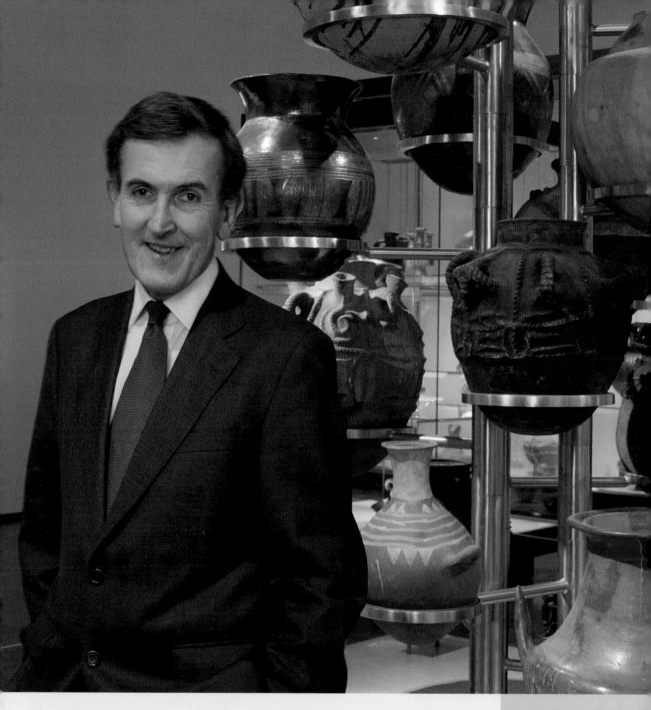

It's a straight trade-off. You can only show the Michelangelo drawings once in a generation if they're still going to be in a good condition in another 500 years. It's my job to arbitrate those trade-offs.

I try to start every day by walking around the galleries in the hours before the visitors arrive at ten o'clock. It's a good way of seeing what's being done, of meeting colleagues and talking to them about their jobs – but it's also really important for me to have some quiet time with the collection. It reminds me what the job is really all about.

to London and reporting on their visit to the British Museum. One German visitor in the 1780s remarked on how surprised he was to find people of all classes going around the collection; even though the numbers of visitors were small, they were very diverse. Numbers have grown as tourism has grown – at the moment we're getting nearly 5 million visitors a year, and of those more than half are from overseas. Almost everyone who comes to London wants to have an experience of it, and most of them are visiting for the first time. Now that London is becoming the world's most international city, our local visiting population is also coming to mirror the global variety of the collection.'

> **It's a place where the neighbourhood can come ... a place where they can bring children**

To its immediate neighbours, those who live and work in central London, the Museum plays a more diverse role. 'There's a sort of village-hall atmosphere to the Museum some-times,' says MacGregor. 'It's a place where the neighbourhood can come that's warm and dry, where they can bring children. We run a lot of family events, activity days, weekends and sleepovers. Some exhibitions address particular parts of the London population, for instance the Bengali community in Camden, the London borough where the Museum is situated.'

As the national collection of the United Kingdom, the Museum also has close links with museums and audiences all over the country. BM exhibitions tour nationwide, and resources are shared in terms of inter-museum loans, conservation and scientific expertise, and research and curatorial support, coordinated through the Museum's Partnership UK programme.

'The British Museum has a special relationship with all other museums in Britain because it was the first one to be set up by Parliament,' says MacGregor. 'It was the beginning of that uniquely British provision of museums free of charge for all citizens, giving access to the personal engagement with the cultures of the world. All the other museums that followed in the nineteenth century are part of that movement and have their roots in the foundation of the British Museum. We take that relationship seriously and actively foster links with museums all over the UK. The BM is a pool of collections and expertise that is the property of the whole country and can be used by all the other museums. For instance, when the Kelvingrove Art Gallery and Museum in Glasgow reopened, they wanted to strengthen their existing Egyptian collection so that they could tell the whole story of ancient Egypt. They came here and had discussions with John Taylor in our department of Ancient Egypt and the Sudan, and the result is a long-term loan of 84 objects, which have been

Opposite: A picture from the *Illustrated London News* of April 1873 showed the popularity of the Museum, which at that time included the Natural History Museum. Below: Today, the Museum encourages an ongoing family atmosphere by running activity events and sleepovers.

seen by 1.3 million visitors in the first three months since Kelvingrove
reopened.'

The British Museum also sends single objects on tour around the country.
Major acquisitions are often made with the support of other museums, and
on occasion the acquisition is shared with other museums. 'When something
big comes into the collection, we like to send it around the country so it can
be seen in different contexts,' says MacGregor. 'The "Queen of the Night"
Babylonian relief [a 4000-year-old terracotta plaque, see page 110] made a
series of weekend stops around the country. The Mold gold cape [a Bronze Age
ceremonial garment] went to Wrexham in 2005 so that it could be seen in the
context of north Wales, where it was found. Then, when it comes back here,

you can see it in the context of the rest of the world – between 1800 and 1750 BC, when it was made.'

These aren't simply ad hoc loans: the Museum has developed an active programme of taking its treasures and expertise out of London to share with the widest-possible national audience. The *Throne of Weapons*, a provocative sculpture from Mozambique made out of decommissioned firearms in 2001, toured 30 venues during 2005–6, including schools, community centres and a prison, raising debate wherever it went. The Olduvai handaxes from Africa are being seen and handled around the country in 2006–7, giving people direct contact with some of the oldest artefacts in the world. When the Lewis Chessmen went on the road, UK audiences had the chance to see some of the BM's biggest stars as part of a touring exhibition of games from around the world. By sharing treasures old and new, the British Museum is making itself a national collection not just in theory but in practice too.

The departure of the British Library in the 1990s allowed for one of the most radical rethinkings of the Museum's disposition of its collection in recent years. The central space around the Reading Room has, of course, been transformed into the Great Court, which has revolutionized visitor access to the collections and finally provided a large public space where people can meet and relax. But the departure of the Library also vacated one of the Museum's most important rooms, the King's Library, completed in 1827, which now houses the Enlightenment Gallery, a collection of objects from many cultures that aims to reflect the mindset and the collecting ethos of the Museum's eighteenth-century founders.

The King's Library is justly regarded as one of the most important neo-classical interiors in the world. Architect Sir Robert Smirke designed it to house a vast collection of books collected by King George III and given to the nation by his rather less literary son King George IV; now it's home to an intriguing museo-logical experiment that marks a deliberate return to the founding principles of the British Museum.

KOZO, THE DOUBLE-HEADED DOG

If I had to pick one image that represents the British Museum's role in the future, it's Kozo, the double-headed dog from the Congo, made in the late nineteenth or early twentieth century. It's an emblem of the unbreakable links that bind the living, the dead and those yet to be born. Dogs were thought to be mediators with the other world, so the two heads look both ways, and in the middle prayers and promises are driven into the body of the animal with nails and blades. The British Museum represents a contract between the past and the future, to keep faith through long stretches of time with the whole of society. The object reminds us very powerfully what we are here to do.

NEIL MACGREGOR, *Director of the BM*

BRENDAN MOORE

Manager of the Enlightenment Gallery

THE MAINTENANCE OF THE COLLECTION in the Enlightenment Gallery is complicated because we have such an extraordinary range of objects. There are bird and mammal skins on loan from the Natural History Museum (NHM), for instance, which require a lot of care; we've developed an insect- and pest-management strategy with the NHM's own conservators. Those specimens are monitored constantly to make sure that beetle and moth larvae don't get in and start eating them. It's a problem that all museums face because where you have organic objects, whether they're animal, botanical or textile, you'll have hungry insects trying to eat them.

The room is cleaned every day by trained cleaning staff. They come in at seven o'clock, cleaning the whole room, making sure that any crumbs from the crisps and sandwiches that people shouldn't have been eating in the first place have been swept up and removed, and getting the gallery ready for opening. That takes two hours every day.

Conservation staff and curators are responsible for the care of the individual objects in the cases. Sometimes we have to move things around, for instance if we're bringing in a large, new object, or if the room is being used for filming or for a function; we regularly stage events for important sponsors and friends of the Museum in the Enlightenment Gallery now. If anything has to be moved across the floor, it's my job to protect it; that's the original 1827 floor of oak and mahogany, and over the years it's been sanded and polished so much that it's a lot thinner than it once was.

We maintain the gallery on a daily basis, but it's not enough to keep everything in pristine condition, so once a year we close the whole room down for a week and give it a thorough overhaul. It's the only gallery in the Museum that closes like that: we've got over 4000 objects in here, and everything has to be inspected for conservation purposes. The largest part of the work in that week revolves around the maintenance of the room itself, and often we work right through the night to get everything done. Changing light bulbs, for instance, is a big job; there's a discreet lighting system hidden away in the alcoves on the top of the windows, and you can't just get up there on a ladder. We have mobile scaffolding towers and hydraulic lifts to get up to the top. There are a lot of windows to clean and a lot of dusting to do.

If we're moving heavy equipment around the room, we have to protect the objects on display. We'll put protective covering on the floor, and we can build boxes round the cases, but the sculpture takes a lot of work. First of all they're wrapped in special conservation tissue, then in polythene, then they're boarded up with cladding. It sounds over the top, but it's a question of risk assessment. We've got people working up at a high level, and there's always a danger that they might drop a tool on to a portrait bust below. Those chaps were very important to the development of the Museum, so we have to take care of them.

Artefacts are usually displayed in their geographic and historic context; in the Enlightenment Gallery, however, objects from all over the world across thousands of years are under one roof, illustrating the intellectual curiosity of the men and women who gave birth to museums all over the world. Objects are reunited for the first time in 250 years: Greek marbles and Assyrian tablets sit next to stuffed animals, brought back into the British Museum from their home at the Natural History Museum.

It's an experiment that quickly found favour with the public, and the Enlightenment Gallery has become one of the most visited rooms in the Museum. 'It's a snapshot of the wider collection,' says BM deputy director Andrew Burnett, who was involved in the project from its inception in the early 1990s, when it became clear that the British Library would be moving out. 'People can come into the room and see at a glance what we've got to offer, which they can then explore in greater depth by moving around the other galleries. But they can also get an idea of the minds that put the Museum together. You get a very strong sense of that magpie mentality, collecting anything interesting that came under its eye. The juxtapositions are extraordinary and, I think, very stimulating.'

Greek vases share space with Islamic amulets; Babylonian cuneiform tablets jostle stuffed animals, prints and medals. Not least among the attractions is the room itself, which is now a venue for events and concerts, as well as housing the collection. 'There's no doubt that Robert Smirke's King's Library is one of the greatest treasures in the Museum,' says Burnett. 'The proportions are absolutely perfect, and you get a wonderful sense of space and order when you walk into it. One of the joys of the project was that it gave us a chance to restore the room to its former glory – but it's not just a beautiful, dead space. It now has an obvious relation to what goes on in the rest of the Museum, which it didn't necessarily have before.'

There's another reason for loving the Enlightenment Gallery, especially in the summer – it's one of the coolest spaces in the Museum, if not in the whole of London, and very handy for the overheated tourist to rest and recover. The air temperature is carefully controlled, and not just for the comfort of visitors: the collection is so diverse and includes so much vulnerable organic material that heat and humidity pose a real danger.

'We have to maintain very strict environmental conditions,' says Brendan Moore, manager of the Enlightenment Gallery. 'We monitor for temperature,

> It's a snapshot of the wider collection ... people can come into the room and see at a glance what we've got to offer

Overleaf: The Enlightenment Gallery, one of the most important neo-classical interiors in Europe, now houses a cross-section of the Museum's diverse collections.

ENLIGHT
DISCOVERING THE WORLD IN

The Enlightenment is the name given to the age of reason, discovery and learning that flourished from about 1680 to 1820 and changed the way that people viewed the world.

Enlightened men and women believed that the key to unlocking the past and the mysteries of the universe lay in directly observing and studying the natural and the man-made world. Their passion for collecting objects, from fossils and flints to Greek vases and ancient scripts, was matched by their desire to impose order

This gallery presents seven imp themes. You can visit them in to follow the themes in sequen The cases along the walls are by type. These help to convey

Gallery guide

ENT

ENTH CENTURY

The objects displayed in this room
were collected during the early years
of the British Museum, which was
founded in 1753. They help us to
explore the passions and ideas of
collectors and scholars at this time.

When the British Museum was founded,
it was a place not only of learning but also of
wonder. This gallery focuses on the Museum's
early collections, recreating that first sense of
amazement and exploring some of the ways
that people in Britain viewed their world
and its past.

HEAD OF A HORSE OF SELENE

This is perhaps the most famous sculpture of the Parthenon in Athens, and one of the most loved pieces in the Museum. The horse (from the eastern pediment and dated around 447–432 BC) has been drawing the chariot of Selene, the moon goddess, across the sky all night, and as dawn breaks and the chariot of the sun god Helios appears, the horse pulls Selene down into the sea. It's a very natural-istic sculpture that vividly captures the wild tension of the exhausted horse, and it's a wonderful example of how a very old piece of stone can seem to be vividly alive.

BRENDAN MOORE, *Manager of the Enlightenment Gallery*

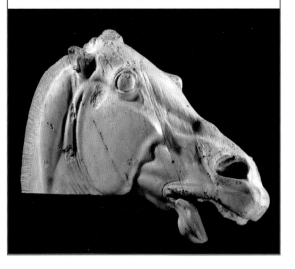

humidity and light. When the gallery was restored, we installed a lot of very twenty-first-century services, all hidden away from view, to control the conditions that the objects are kept in. In the basement beneath that beautiful, original floor there's a huge amount of heavy-duty plant, which keeps everything cool and dry. It's beautiful and serene upstairs, but downstairs it looks like the interior of a nuclear submarine.'

The British Museum is one of the greatest visitor attractions in the world – but how is that great machine of culture kept in good working order? How does the Museum sustain the kind of wear and tear that is the inevitable consequence of its popularity? That's a question addressed on a daily basis by the hard-services team, who look after all aspects of museum maintenance, from cleaning the enormous roof of the Great Court to monitoring tiny fluctuations in temperature or humidity in a display cabinet.

A team of managers, engineers, joiners, carpenters, decorators and handymen cover every aspect of museum maintenance, all under the watchful eye of Derek Martin, the Hard-services Facilities manager, 'which is a modern way of saying I'm the chief engineer and maintenance manager.' 'Hard services' covers everything to do with the fabric of the building, from the concrete that holds the railings in place right through to the information technology that controls heating, fire alarms, air conditioning and lifts. They'll even do the heavier cleaning, although the day-to-day cleaning of the Museum is taken care of by their sister team, soft services.

Hard-services jobs divide into two main areas – those that are necessitated by the day-to-day running of the Museum and those that are planned in advance. 'The reactive side of our work can be just about anything,' says Martin. 'We go on a daily walkabout round the galleries to see if any paint

I CAME TO THE BRITISH MUSEUM IN 2005 after working for years as a contract manager for the government and for stockbrokers in the City. I'd never been to the British Museum before in my life! I'm an engineer, so old bits of stone don't interest me very much. I haven't got a clue about the value or importance of most of the things in the Museum, and I very rarely look into the showcases because I'm busy thinking about whether the seals are working, whether the alarm system is working, that sort of thing. But I'm starting to get an idea of how important this place is to people. When I saw thousands of people queuing up for the Michelangelo exhibition, crowding around one tiny bit of paper in a glass case, I realized that those objects have a real significance to people, which has obviously passed me by.

That makes it a very good place to work in. I always say to the engineers, 'Look, whenever you get fed up with your job – which we all do from time to time – go out into the forecourt on any day, around lunchtime, and look at all the people. See the kids running around on the grass, look at all the people enjoying themselves and realize what a special place you're working in.' This job is about human beings and what's really important to them, and you'll never replicate that in Whitehall or Canary Wharf. Just walking through the galleries, seeing the people looking at the objects, is brilliant. Whenever I have a meeting with another department, I always take the long way round to get there just so I can see the Museum in action.

The working culture within the Museum is really different. In the commercial world, or in government, you tend to get bolshy people who are bored with their own jobs, and so they decide to muscle in on mine. Here, they're essentially scholars and academics, and while they can be a little strange, with that strangeness comes a desire to let you get on with your job while they get on with theirs. The thing is that they all really love working here. They enjoy their jobs, and that enables me to enjoy mine. They say good morning to you in the corridor; they bend over backwards to help you, and that is so refreshing.

When I first arrived at the British Museum, I had to go to a little team-building, motivational-training thing with a group of about 20 people. During the introductions, everyone said how long they'd been working here, and by the time it got to my turn they'd already totted up about 300 years among them. I was astounded. I've never known that in my industry. In the engineering contractors' world, human resources departments consider it a success if they have people who stay in one place for over 12 months! Here we've got people who are pushing 40 years.

My friends and my partner were amazed when I got this job; it seems that they'd all been visiting the British Museum since they were kids. I'm surprised how many people feel a close connection with it. Lots of people have said to me, 'I'm really glad to say I have a friend who runs this place!', and that makes me feel very proud.

DEREK MARTIN

Manager of Hard-services Facilities

needs touching up, or a light bulb needs replacing. We take about 1000 calls a month for various problems like blocked toilets, graffiti on cherrywood doors, flickering lights, broken tiles or whatever. Sometimes people will kick a barrier and pull it out of the concrete. We have very large doors on the middle floors, and they often get damaged by people slamming them.'

The more proactive side of the team's work involves planned maintenance of all the major areas of the Museum at least once a year. 'We try to give the common areas, like the corridors and staircases, a thorough servicing every six months,' says Martin. 'The larger galleries we do on an annual basis. That has to be scheduled in advance; there are 81 galleries to maintain, as well as all the backstage stuff like the student rooms, store rooms, offices and curatorial departments. Planning that work can be hard because sometimes you can be knocking on a door for weeks, only to find that the entire curatorial department has gone to China. Elsewhere in the engineering industry it's very much nine to five, but here we don't have regular office hours. We can't just go into an office at 5 p.m. expecting it to be empty.'

Gallery maintenance involves a variety of skills, from decorating and mending windows to installing and upgrading sophisticated electronic monitoring equipment. The galleries are fully equipped with fire alarms and intruder alarms, and on top of that there's a whole battery of equipment that monitors the conditions in which the objects are kept. 'Climate control is one of the things that takes up a lot of my time,' says Martin. 'All of the cases have little refrigeration units built into them, and although the tolerances aren't that fine, they must be maintained. If a seal breaks, the air gets in and an object gets wet – and if it's organic material, that's a real problem. We have to make sure that metal objects aren't being tarnished by sulphur, so we have air filters. The expertise isn't ours – that's the job of the conservators and scientists – but it's up to us to keep it all working.

'If anything goes wrong, it's picked up by the sensors, and an alarm goes off on one of the monitoring systems. They not only flash up on computer screens throughout the engineering department, but also go through to a modem with an auto-dialler, so a text message can be sent to the engineers wherever they are. That happens within seconds of a sensor picking up a problem, even at night. The engineer on duty has to get out of bed, phone up the night-security team to say he's coming in and get here as fast as he can. There's usually a certain amount of leeway; it's not like a data centre, for instance, where they don't give you five minutes. Here we usually have a few hours. But if something is rated Priority One, we can get to it very fast.

Cleaning around one of the Museum's most precious objects, the Rosetta stone.

Everything in the 2006 Michelangelo exhibition, for instance, was rated Priority One.'

The biggest job of all for Derek Martin and his team is the maintenance of the Great Court, a huge space with highly specialized cleaning and maintenance requirements. The first priority is to protect the objects on display in the Great Court, many of them large pieces of sculpture that can't be easily moved. The carpenters go in first to build protective boxing around them, followed by engineers with access equipment. The standard piece of equipment is a MEWP – a mobile elevated work platform – that's basically a little crane on a track that can move around the space giving access to higher levels. 'But they have to be very light,' says Martin, 'because the floor of the Great Court is made of marble, and it will only take about 1 tonne per 2 square metres. So the

MEWP has to be on a fine line between the maximum reach and the maximum weight. Unfortunately, that means we can't reach the ceiling because something that can go that high would weigh far too much and would damage the floor. We can only get three-quarters of the way up.'

The solution? Abseilers, of course. The star performers of Derek Martin's team can swing around in the interior of the Great Court, reaching the parts that other engineers cannot reach. 'They climb up the side, latch themselves on to something, run ropes across and then swing around all day long. They can install bird netting, or attach promotional banners, or clean the glass of the roof. It's cheaper, quicker and safer to get them up there than it would be to get cranes to reach up from the floor.'

The outside of the Great Court roof also requires specialist cleaning skills. There are 3312 individual panes of glass, each of a unique shape, held in place by 5200 steel members welded into 1800 nodes. That's not a job for someone with a bucket and a squeegee. 'You can't walk unaided on the roof,' says Martin. 'You have to be hooked on by a harness to a network of cables that runs over the roof, which can't be seen from below. The cleaners have to be light! They get up there, hook themselves on and away they go. It takes about two weeks to clean the whole roof, and we do it every three months because being in the centre of London it gets very dirty. We use demineralized water so that there's no limescale build-up.'

> **3312 individual panes of glass ... That's not a job for someone with a bucket and a squeegee**

There are some more low-tech ways of keeping the roof clean; every week or so a Harris hawk called Emu is flown around the area to discourage the pigeons from getting a foothold. But not all birds are as easily scared off. 'The main problem at the moment seems to be with seagulls,' says Martin. 'Not just for the obvious reason of making a mess on the roof; they're nesting up there, and for some reason they're dying up there as well. One theory is that they mistake the curved forms of the roof for the surface of the sea: the glass has a blue-green tint, and it reflects the light in a way that might make it look like water. We think the seagulls might see the surface and then see the little people moving around underneath, mistake them for a shoal of herring and dive down. They think they're going to get a tasty meal, but in fact they're aiming at a group of schoolkids – and then, bang!'

2

All human life passes through those doors

The British Museum opens its doors to nearly 5 million visitors a year.
They come from all over the world and from just around the corner. Local
people use the Museum as a meeting and eating place; they pop in to
spend 20 minutes with a favourite object; they attend talks and performances,
or use the extensive education facilities. Visitors to London usually have the
British Museum somewhere near the top of their 'must-see' list. A visit to the
BM is part of the experience of 'doing' London, and in return for that global
interest and loyalty the Museum strives to provide levels of intellectual access
and enjoyment for the widest possible range of visitors. School parties might
want to get to the mummies as quickly as they can, then find a convenient
space in which to eat their packed lunches. Scholars want to study the
collections or consult the curators. Tourists on a tight schedule want to tick
off the treasures before going on to the next destination. For all those needs
and many more, the British Museum has to provide facilities,
information and answers.

All the Museum staff, from the security guards on the
front gate onwards, are ready to answer visitors' questions
and help them to get the most out of their visit. Plans, maps,
leaflets and signage are available every step of the way, and
for many visitors the first port of call is the information desk
in the Great Court, permanently staffed and ready to deal
with every conceivable question, from 'Where are the
toilets?' to 'Is this coin I found in my back garden worth
anything?' When Neil MacGregor joined the British Museum
as director in 2002, he spent a day in a blue shirt working
on the information desk. As he sat there giving directions
and handing out leaflets, he became aware of a woman
watching him from a few yards away. Eventually she
approached the desk and asked, 'Aren't you Neil MacGregor,
the former director of the National Gallery?' MacGregor
confirmed that he was, much to the woman's shocked surprise; she thought
he'd been demoted!

The story of the Museum over the centuries has been one of ever-
increasing access. When the BM first opened its doors in 1759, public access
was extremely limited, with a complicated system of invitations. Would-be
visitors had to apply for a ticket from the hall porter, and even then they were
admitted only with the approval of the principal librarian. An early visit to the
Museum was a hurried affair, with groups of 15 rushed around by a member

Above: Ben Murrell
at work on one of the
information desks in the
Great Court.
Opposite: Security staff
get ready both to help
the public and protect
the collection.

MICKEY MOUTOU

Supervisor of Visitor
Operations

I CAME TO THE BRITISH MUSEUM IN 1978, when I was 24 years old. I'd recently got married, and I needed a job, so I just walked in off the street, went to the personnel department and asked them if there were any vacancies. I had an interview straight away and got a job as a gallery assistant. I've been here ever since; it'll be 30 years before you know it. Since then I've worked in every gallery in the Museum, and now I'm a supervisor of visitor operations, which means that I control a team across several galleries.

My dad used to work here as well, he was an assistant in the British Library, and he'd always been trying to get me to work there, but I said I'd never do it. I never dreamed that I'd end up being here for nearly the whole of my working life. In those days, the working conditions were very different, and there was no training. You were given a map of the Museum and off you went. You had to learn everything on the job.

The Museum is my second home, and I still love being here after all these years. My day starts at about nine o'clock, when we're briefed by the manager in the operations office, who tells us of any special problems, like toilets being out of order or galleries being closed. I brief the team, and then I spend the rest of the day making sure that everything is running smoothly and responding to the needs of the visitors and the staff. No two days are the same; we'll do anything from changing a light bulb to telling the visitors about the exhibits. I really like a challenge; the more I've got to do, the happier I am.

The biggest change in the Museum since I've been here was the opening of the Great Court. It's made it much easier for the visitors to get around, and it's certainly improved the quality of my working life. We never had any big, open spaces before, and it could get a bit claustrophobic sometimes. I was lucky enough to see the whole building process, from the demolition of the old book stacks right through to the final construction of the roof. I sponsored a pane of glass in the roof in memory of my dad, who passed away.

When the Queen opened the Great Court, we had a chance to put on the Windsor livery, which we're entitled to wear on special occasions. It was granted to the Museum by William IV in 1835, and it consists of a blue coat with a scarlet collar and cuffs and the words British Museum engraved around the buttons. I've seen all the royal family come to visit, except the Queen Mother, and it's always a great honour to put on the Windsor livery.

of staff, forbidden from stopping and 'gazing at objects'. 'We had no time allowed to examine any thing,' complained one visitor in 1817. 'Our conductor pushed on without minding questions, or unable to answer them, but treating the company with *double entendres* and witticisms on various subjects in natural history, in a style of vulgarity and impudence.'

Gradually, however, the Museum accepted that everyone wanted to get in, particularly as the collection was maintained at public expense. The principal librarian, Henry Ellis, complained in 1835 that 'people of a higher grade would hardly wish to come to the Museum at the same time with sailors from the dock-yards and girls whom they might bring with them,' but by then the Museum was operating an open admissions policy. Ever since, sailors from the dockyards (and their girls) have been welcome, as have people from every other walk of life. The collection represents cultures from all over the world, created by and for people of every degree from peasant to emperor; it's important that the universality of the collection is reflected in the way it's presented to its global public.

Care, however, must still be taken. Security guards are permanently deployed at the front gates, the main entrance, the north entrance, the front hall and in the Great Court. Thereafter, the main interface between the visitors and the Museum is the gallery assistants (or 'warders', as they used to be known), who work in every gallery, keeping an eye on the safety of the collection and the well-being of the visitors, prepared to answer questions whenever necessary.

'People often think it must be the most boring job in the world,' says Mickey Moutou, Visitor Operations supervisor, who's worked as a gallery assistant throughout the Museum. 'They think we just stand there staring at the same objects, day in, day out. Nothing could be further from the truth; it's a very busy, varied job, and you're dealing with a huge range of demands all the time. People want directions, of course, but they also want to know about the objects in the galleries. Sometimes they want to discuss issues, and the gallery assistants have got to have a ready answer. We can't really get into a one-to-one discussion about the Elgin marbles, for example, because you inevitably get a crowd gathering, and then everyone wants to say their bit. The gallery would come to a standstill!'

> People often think it must be the most boring job in the world … nothing could be further from the truth

Gallery assistants move around the Museum on a regular rota so that after their basic training and a few weeks shadowing an experienced colleague on the job they're ready for whatever the visitors can throw at them. Some-times, with major exhibitions or around particularly popular objects, such as the Rosetta stone, the job is largely crowd control. The safety of the collection is paramount, and the gallery assistants often have to remind people not to touch or climb on objects.

'You'd be surprised how often people have an urge to jump up on some-thing that clearly isn't meant to be touched,' says Moutou. 'Some 98 per cent of

visitors understand perfectly how to behave in a museum and have a great deal of respect for the objects, but there's always a few who like to misbehave. We just ask them very politely not to.'

There's always a few who like to misbehave. We just ask them very politely not to

The addition of the Great Court in 2000 has revolutionized the way in which the Museum 'processes' its visitors. Access to all the galleries has been made much simpler; anyone who visited the Museum before 2000 will remember the labyrinthine route that took you, say, to the Egyptian galleries. Now, instead of going into the congested front hall, then going up, along, down, around and across, you can access most of the galleries by a relatively short walk that cuts across the Great Court. When the British Library occupied the Reading

Room and had its book stacks all around, public access was, to say the least, compromised. It could take up to 15 minutes to get to the mummies.

'The Great Court has made our job so much easier,' says Moutou. 'I used to spend half my time rattling off the directions to the Egyptian galleries: through the postcard gallery, right through Lower Egyptian, up the west stairs, turn left and so on. It's much easier now – but the only problem is that the Great Court is so popular it's increased the number of visitors. When the Reading Room was there you didn't really see the volume, but now, if you stand in the Great Court for ten minutes, you see just how many people are passing through the building.'

The volume and variety of visitors is a challenge at every level of the Museum, from practical people-management through to more abstract notions

Opposite: Mickey Moutou helping a visitor. Every member of the Museum staff is ready to answer questions and to give guidance.
 Above: The Egyptian galleries are probably the most popular destination for both children and adults.

THE RAFFLES GAMELAN

My favourite object in the Museum, for entirely personal reasons, is the Raffles gamelan. A gamelan is a set of musical instruments from Indonesia, and it's something that I've been playing for a long time, both at home and in Java and Bali. This is one of the oldest gamelans in Europe, and certainly the most beautiful, and I was really excited when I started working at the British Museum to know that it was here. It was brought back to England by Sir Stamford Raffles, former Lieutenant-governor of Java and founder of Singapore, so it has a really interesting provenance. It came out on exhibition a few years ago, but it's not on permanent display. I would do anything for a chance to play it.

XERXES MAZDA, *Head of Learning and Audience*

of intellectual access and interpretation of objects. 'All human life passes through those doors,' says Xerxes Mazda, head of Learning and Audience. 'That's what makes the British Museum a unique challenge. Here the interest is as diverse as the collection. In addition, you have the tourism aspect: the BM is world famous, and it's part of the experience of coming to Britain.'

The challenge, in essence, lies in getting people to where they want to go – or, if they don't know where they want to go, getting them to a place that will give them the quality of experience they hoped for when they came through the doors. Some visitors are easy: they know their way around the collections and can go straight to their destination, spend an hour looking at a few choice objects, take as much or as little as they want from the information that's provided alongside and go away fulfilled. But those people account for a tiny percentage of the Museum's visitors.

'We have to address the key needs of people who might be coming here for the first or only time in their life,' says Mazda. 'They might have a whole day here or just an hour. We have to find different ways of telling them how to get the most out of their visit. We have to be very clear what the offer is. Firstly, we've got to say, "We cover the whole world." Secondly, we have to tell them, "We don't have paintings here." After that, there's a whole layer of information about how the galleries are arranged – by country, by civilization and so on – so that you can find your way to what interests you. We're constantly looking at new ways of setting out our wares at the start of the visit.'

A recognition of the many and varied reasons for visiting the British Museum lies at the heart of the way in which objects, galleries and exhibitions are presented. With a collection of that size, containing several million objects, all with a story to tell and some insight to offer into the history of human civilization, it's obviously impossible for every visitor to engage fully with everything.

'There used to be an idea that you could measure the "success" of a museum by how long people spent in front of objects and how many facts they recalled,' says Mazda, 'but now there's a recognition that people judge the experience in many different ways. Our role now, I think, is to tell people that it's OK to approach the collection in any way that works for them. We still have a lot of visitors who try to "do" the whole Museum in two hours, and they start panicking when they realize that there are over 80 galleries. They end up walking through a gallery, glancing from side to side and taking nothing in. Or they'll run up to something, take a photograph and then run off. It's like photocopying as a substitute for reading.

> We still have a lot of visitors who try to 'do' the whole Museum in two hours

'Our job to some degree is to slow people down, to say, "It's OK to see only a tiny part of the Museum. Just look at five things – relax!" We do that in a number of different ways. We have guided tours that take visitors around a selection of the key objects in the collection, or to one gallery for an "eye-opener" tour that focuses on a few things in depth. That slows people down; you give them a bite-size amount of information that they can digest and enjoy. Nobody can ever hope to get round the whole Museum on one visit, and I want to get that message across loud and clear from the moment people come in the doors.'

The way in which visitors use the British Museum is gauged through continuous research. Sometimes a selection of visitors will be invited to take part in a focus group. Sometimes researchers will take to the floor with clip-boards and do on-the-spot interviews with visitors to find out how an individual visit is going. Observational research tracks visitor movements: the time spent in front of particular objects, the most popular galleries and so on. All this information is directing and influencing the way that the British Museum pre-sents its collection, particularly when designing a new exhibition or redesigning an existing gallery. The impact can be seen clearly in the labelling and other interpretation of objects using a wide range of media.

'People have an idea that a label has always existed alongside an object,' says Richard Parkinson, assistant Keeper in the department of Ancient Egypt and the Sudan. 'In fact, the interpretation of objects changes all the time; it's contingent on the moral and political climate, and the demands of the visitors. The ancient objects that we have on show here came out of the ground with no "meaning" at all; it's up to successive generations to reinterpret them for them-selves. Fifty years ago, academics at the Museum took a much more censorious attitude to issues like sexuality. Now people want to explore those issues and learn about how they were reflected in ancient cultures. We can't censor the past. If we are a repository for the memories of mankind, we have a responsibility to be honest and egalitarian about the way we interpret those memories.'

The labelling of objects tends now to be more discursive, engaging with issues much wider than an object's narrow historical provenance. And as technology has become cheaper, it's being used more and more in galleries and exhibitions. 'On-screen information used to be aimed almost entirely at children,' says Xerxes Mazda, 'but now that nearly everyone is familiar with the internet, they're much more likely to engage with that kind of technology. So we're offering more screen-based material, which gives people another way of exploring objects. You can use the British Museum website as a way of preparing for your visit, researching the things you want to see in advance, or of deepening the value of your visit when you get home, finding out more about the objects that you've seen and exploring them in a different way. We're really only at the beginning of that process, but it's already clear that the internet is giving visitors a whole new level of access to the collections.'

... the internet is giving visitors a whole new level of access to the collections

Nothing can replace personal engagement with the objects, however. 'It's important never to lose sight of how powerful these objects are,' says Irving Finkel, assistant Keeper in the department of the Middle East. 'You could look at one object for hours and hours and never get to the bottom of it. If you come to the Museum as a visitor, it's easy to let your eye slide over things, even something as obviously brilliant and complex as the Assyrian lion-hunt reliefs [a captivating series of seventh-century BC stone relief sculptures showing a royal lion hunt]. If you were imprisoned with one of those reliefs for 24 hours, it would never get boring. There are a thousand details. All the sculptures in the series have that quality, and that's just one set of objects. It's difficult to balance the needs of the visitors with the power and significance of every individual object.'

One way of enabling visitors to engage more fully with the collection is the hands-on programme, run throughout the Museum by volunteers. A group of objects is selected by the curators to form a handling collection. Trained volunteers working in the galleries help visitors to learn more about these objects through handling – and the programme has been a huge success since its introduction in 2001.

'It started as the idea of a curator in the Coins and Medals department,' says Kusuma Barnett, head of the Volunteer Programme at the British Museum. 'He felt that people might get more out of coins by being able to hold them; after all, that's what they're designed for. Often the idea in museums is

"Look, but don't touch!", so this was a very different way for people to engage with objects. We had thousands of people coming to handle the coins – children in particular seem to love it – and now there are six handling stations all around the Museum. Until you've tried it, you've no idea of the difference it makes. Take handaxes, for instance. If you look at them in a case, they just look like lumps of stone, and it's hard to get very excited about them unless you're a specialist. But they're some of the oldest man-made objects in the world; the ones from the Olduvai Gorge in Tanzania are 1.5 to 2 million years old. When you hold one of these axes you feel as if you have contact with someone from the past. If you can feel the weight, the shape of it, you get a better understanding of how it was made and used. It is a wonderful experience. When Prince Charles came to the opening of the Enlightenment Gallery he was absolutely enthralled. It was difficult to get him away from the handling desk.'

Above: Kusuma Barnett (left), the head of the Volunteer Programme, at one of the popular handling stations in the Enlightenment Gallery.

When you hold one of these axes you feel as if you have contact with someone from the past

KUSUMA BARNETT

Head of the Volunteer Programme

THE BRITISH MUSEUM has a group of about 350 volunteers who work in different capacities all over the Museum. Some of them are behind the scenes, doing administrative work for the various departments; others work with the public doing things like object-handling sessions, eye-opener tours, helping out with events, taking tickets and so on.

My responsibility is to look after the whole Volunteer Programme, recruit and train volunteers, and make sure that they are all happy and the programme is running smoothly. The Museum has a reputation around the whole world, so there are a lot of people who want to get involved. Many are retired people who came here a lot in their working lives and want to give something back. Then we get hundreds of students, who are looking for work experience and might want to go into museum work. Most people volunteer because they are interested in part of the collection. My challenge sometimes is to move them outside their particular area of interest and encourage them to work in a new department; it's a great opportunity to learn – you might never get the chance again.

People come from far and wide. Some live just round the corner; some live on the other side of the world. One retired American gentleman stays in his flat in London between April and October, when he works here; then he goes back to the USA for the winter. Some young people in full-time work give us their spare time, which always amazes me. One young woman who was a student volunteer gave it up when she started doing her law degree, but she missed it so much she came back and now gives us one Sunday a month.

We have lots of people applying to become volunteers. Sadly, we can't take all of them. I'm a volunteer myself, although I come in five days a week. I've been here since 1989; it started off as one day a week, then two, and now I'm full time. My husband laughs at me because I left my previous job to be a lady of leisure, and now I'm doing this. It started when I wanted to sign up to become a Friend of the British Museum, and I couldn't find anyone to help me. Eventually I found someone and said, 'You should have a desk, possibly manned by volunteers, where people can join the Friends.' To this day I don't know why I said that. A few weeks later, I had a phone call: 'You know that desk you suggested? We've decided to open it, and we'd like you to help with it.' In 2001 the Museum wanted someone to take on a proper coordination role, and ever since then I've been here full time. In 2006 I was awarded an MBE for services to museums. I was very excited to receive it, of course, but even more thrilled by the Museum's public acknowledgement of the contribution the volunteers make. The whole day went in a bit of a blur, but I must say it was superbly organized. I was very nervous, but the Palace staff were very reassuring: 'Don't worry if you do it wrong – the Queen will know what to do.' Afterwards, to celebrate, I met up with a group of volunteers for lunch. After all, it was as much their award as mine.

Handling stations, on-screen interpretation and guided tours are just some of the ways in which the British Museum adds value to its visitors' experience of the collection. But there are other developments that, in their quiet way, are doing just as much to revolutionize the experience of museum-visiting. The Asahi Shimbun displays are housed in a small gallery, about 10 × 7 metres, just inside the main entrance. Since 2005, the gallery has been used for temporary displays that highlight particular objects from the collection in a new context. The first exhibition in there featured ancient African handaxes; subsequent displays have included prints by Rembrandt, the Warren cup (see page 140) and the Royal Game of Ur (see page 102).

'I like to think of this room as the Museum's play-space,' says J. D. Hill, the curator in charge of these displays. 'We can experiment with new ways of presenting objects and learn from our experiences, or even get it wrong. We can offer the visitors a quick, one-stop experience that changes on a regular basis.'

The first exhibition in the gallery featured those ever popular quartz handaxes from the Olduvai Gorge. 'In essence, we took three rather dull-looking bits of stone that just happen to be the oldest human artefacts in the collection and some of the oldest humanly made things in the world. Usually when museums display objects like these the eye skims over them. We put them in a special display case and lit them as if they were the most priceless jewels in a jeweller's shop in Bond Street! They looked gorgeous; the light reflected off the cut surfaces, it shone through the stone, and people were transfixed. It made them stop, look and think. That exhibition transformed those handaxes into the iconic images from the collection they deserve to be, and will inform the way they are shown from now on.'

Creating new icons for the Museum is a serious business; it's necessary to divert the attention of visitors away from the obvious, congested areas. 'As soon as you take something out of its usual display, you're changing the way people look at it, and by doing that you're changing or adding to its meaning,' says Hill. 'This gallery is a workshop for new

THE GREAT TORC OF SNETTISHAM

I'm extremely fond of the Snettisham torc. It's one of those objects that we don't know a great deal about, and that excites me. It is quite large, made from a kilogram of gold, and incredibly beautiful; the workmanship is quite complex. The fact we don't know for certain who owned it or how it was used fascinates me. Mysteries make objects come alive for us. We have a replica of the torc that we once used in a handling session, and I have worn it sometimes. I must say, it looked rather good.

KUSUMA BARNETT, *Head of the Volunteer Programme*

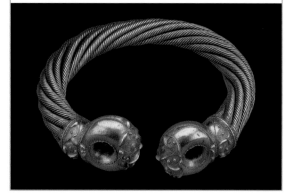

STONE HANDAXE

The handaxes from the Olduvai Gorge in Tanzania are between 1.5 and 2 million years old. An object of this indescribable age surviving and being on display in the building where I work is breathtaking. Handaxes have been used during the handling sessions for blind audiences. It's magnificent that the Museum provides opportunities for people with little or no sight to touch an object that is so inconceivably ancient; that you can hold something so old, made by human hands, and envisage how it was used is remarkable. It's a link to our very earliest ancestors, and it enables us to understand more about the way they lived. It's made of quartz, which is quite hard to work, so the craftsman was obviously very skilled. It's beautiful to look at, a real work of art.

JANE SAMUELS, *Access Manager*

ways of presenting objects, and because it's a small space, people aren't going to rush through. We only really want them to look at a couple of things. We're not bombarding them with information. We're experimenting a lot with the balance of text to object. Traditionally, curators want people to read a big text panel first, then look at the object with all that information in their minds. We know from research that people don't do that; they look at the object first, and if it grabs them, they might read a bit of the text. And nobody but the most dedicated visitor reads the introductory panels. In this room we're cutting back on text panels and writing slightly longer labels that go beside the objects. We can focus those labels on the specific issues and ideas that we're trying to explore.'

An example of this focused approach to object display was an exhibition in summer 2006 built around the Warren cup, a first-century AD Roman silver drinking vessel decorated with scenes of men having sex. The cup was in a special central case, and against the walls were four small cases containing other objects relating to sexuality in the ancient Greek and Roman world. In addition, there were some images of drawings and prints that revealed the reaction of later cultures to homosexuality, including a blow-up from the 2005 film *Brokeback Mountain*.

'The purpose of that exhibition was twofold,' says Hill. 'Firstly, we wanted to bestow a sort of iconic status on the Warren cup because it's a very important object that we felt needed to be put in the spotlight. Secondly, we wanted to show that the Museum is proactively engaged in debates about things like sexuality. We're not just passively showing old objects in a traditional, fuddy-duddy way. We're taking contentious, topical subjects and relating them not just to how people lived and thought in the ancient world, but also to how we live and think now. The exhibition asked a lot of questions – and the people who went to it came out asking even more. One thing we've learnt from the gallery is that questions are much more interesting to visitors than answers.'

The potential for the gallery is vast. 'We're learning how to create a buzz around certain objects, and that never ceases to surprise me. Over Lent and Easter 2006 we put two Rembrandt prints of the Crucifixion on display. I didn't think it would work; I thought it was too dark and too stark. But it was one of the most successful things we've done in there. We were asking people to compare two pictures – and they did! They spent a lot of time in front of them, and the atmosphere was very calm and contemplative. If you walk around the Museum, you'll realize how hard it is to create that kind of mood.'

> We're learning how to create a buzz around certain objects

While the public galleries are constantly being monitored and revised in order to maximize enjoyment and engagement, there's another level of access behind the scenes that allows visitors to deal directly with the Museum's curatorial staff and get up close and personal with some of the most precious objects in the collection. The curatorial departments have a study room, where visitors can go to look at objects – anything from a clock or a coin to a Michelangelo drawing. In addition, they can talk to the experts – there's a curator on duty in every department every day, ready to answer questions about objects or to make referrals for more expert advice.

Say, for instance, you're interested in clocks. You might have an old family heirloom that you want to know more about. You might be studying the history of clocks and want to look at an example of a certain type of mechanism. You might simply want to sit and marvel at one of the hundreds of beautiful, old timepieces that are not on permanent display. 'All you have to do is telephone to make an appointment,' says David Thompson, head of Horology. 'We prefer people to ring up first so that we can prepare a bit. After that, you have secure and supervised access to the entire collection. We don't allow people to dismantle clocks and watches, but we're happy to let them have a good look inside things.'

This sort of engagement happens all over the Museum. Metal detectorists turn up with coins that they've found in a field. Gardeners arrive with objects that they've unearthed in a flower bed. The range of questions and objects that come to the information desk is so wide that the curators are stretched way beyond their particular field of expertise. 'I'm a Greek vase specialist,' says Dyfri Williams, Keeper of the department of Greek and Roman Antiquities, 'but working here you have to go way beyond your speciality. If you're on the duty rota, you might have to answer a question about a Roman gemstone, or a Greek bronze or a sculpture. Someone could turn up at the information desk with a statue they've inherited from Aunt Sally, and they want to know more about it. Often it's rubbish, of course, but you never know.

'A fragment of pottery was brought in not so long ago; I took one look at it and immediately realized that it was not where it should have been. I made a call to a small museum in the UK, and it turned out that there had been a theft that they didn't know about. The man who brought it here had bought it at auction – and he immediately returned it to the museum where it belonged. At other times, I've had calls from lawyers saying that there's an object in a client's will that's described as "a Grecian urn", and they want to know what it's worth for probate purposes. They bring it in, you turn it over, and it's stamped on the bottom "Made in Athens". It's a mixed bag, but it's very good training for curators to learn how to recognize things quickly. And it's important for the Museum as a public body to be able to answer questions; that's one of the fundamental principles of public access.'

Perhaps the most surprising aspect of this open-door policy is the study room of the department of Prints and Drawings, where, more or less at the touch of a button, you can find yourself face to face with priceless works on paper by the Old Masters, in one of the most beautiful rooms London has to offer. The department of Prints and Drawings contains work from the early Renaissance right up to the present day, and most of it cannot be on permanent display because of its sensitivity to light. But students and other art enthusiasts need only turn up in order to see anything they want.

'You show some form of identification at the front desk, you're shown in, you request whatever you'd like to see, from Michelangelo to Tracey Emin, and within five or ten minutes it could be brought out for you by one of the study-room staff,' says Hugo Chapman, a curator in the department. 'We can accommodate up to 12 people at a time, but frequently there are only three or four. We don't have an appointment system; it's on a first-come, first-served basis.'

There are a few obvious rules in the study room: food, drink and pens are all banned (pencils only!), and for group visits there will be a Perspex screen protecting the objects. 'Obviously these works on paper are very fragile and light sensitive,' says Chapman, 'and it would be easier to look after them if we never, ever took them out of their folders. Many other museums round the world put up barriers between the public and their collections; you have to have all sorts of credentials and letters from

> ... you request whatever you'd like to see, from Michelangelo to Tracey Emin, and within five or ten minutes it could be brought out for you

distinguished professors before you're allowed anywhere near. But these drawings belong not just to the Museum but to the world, and it's central to the ethos of the Museum that people should be able to look at them.'

The resources of the Museum – scholarship, design, interpretation, organization – play a part in the major exhibitions that keep it in the headlines. As a world-class institution, the British Museum can ask for material from most of the major collections to supplement its own substantial holdings – but volume and value of exhibits isn't enough to make a successful show. 'We always bear

Above: The study room of the department of Prints and Drawings, where students have access to works ranging from Michelangelo to Tracey Emin.

BRONZE HEAD OF APOLLO (THE CHATSWORTH HEAD)

The Chatsworth Apollo is a fifth-century BC bronze head that was, for a long time, in the possession of the dukes of Devonshire at Chatsworth House in Derbyshire. It came here to the BM in 1958. To me it encapsulates the idealized beauty of classical art that was such an important inspiration to Renaissance artists. Whenever I look at it, I like to think about how wonderful the entire figure must have been.

HUGO CHAPMAN, *Curator of Prints and Drawings, Italian School pre-1880*

in mind that you can still make a bad exhibition out of good material,' says Xerxes Mazda of the Learning and Audience department. 'Our job is to make sure that visitors enjoy themselves and get as much as possible out of the material. You can't just stick hundreds of things in cases with labels beside them and hope for the best.'

In 2006 the Museum produced *Michelangelo Drawings: Closer to the Master*, the first major Michelangelo show at the BM for over 30 years. Everyone knew it was going to be a big draw; Michelangelo is one of the few names in art that guarantees a sell-out. But how could the Museum ensure access on all levels? And how could it reinterpret the work of Michelangelo for a generation who had never seen it before?

'We have to address the issues on so many different levels,' says Mazda. 'First of all, there's the very basic issue of getting large numbers of people in and out comfortably and safely in a way that will allow them to engage with the work. The challenge of all the big shows that we put on here at the British Museum is the sheer number of people who will come. If you love Michelangelo, what you really want to do is stand alone in front of the work and contemplate it. That will obviously never be possible in an exhibition of this nature, but we have to find ways of managing the experience so that it's as rewarding as possible. Some of that we address through design – simple things, such as looking at visitor flow and designing the space accordingly. We know, for instance, that people tend to move slowly through the first couple of rooms in a big exhibition, then they speed up – so we made those initial spaces much larger so they wouldn't be congested.'

After those basic logistics have been addressed, it's up to the curator, the designer and the interpreters to work out what, exactly, they want to put across to the public. 'The first question I ask of the curator is "What's the story?",' says Mazda. 'The curators have objects with hundreds of different meanings attached to them, but what we need to present to the visitors is one cogent story that they can follow through. That gives a shape to the exhibition, and it dictates the design to a great extent. It's at that point, once the basic shape is in place, that the curator, the designers and the interpreters get to work on captions, panels and interactive material.'

In the case of Michelangelo, curator Hugo Chapman had a very clear storyline in mind: he wanted to find out what the artist's drawings told us about his life. 'It was a very biographical show,' says Chapman. 'My criterion for selecting a piece was always "What does this tell us about how Michelangelo lived, how he thought, what he believed and felt?" With an artist as prolific as Michelangelo, you can't just bundle together a few hundred great works and hope they'll speak for themselves. You have to impose a kind of narrative on them. In this case, the work tells us a great deal about the artist's life because we have so much supplementary information in the form of letters and Michelangelo's poetry. We can trace a correlation between what he was reading, who he was in love with, where the money was coming from, and the kind of work that he produced. There's actually so much material about Michelangelo that I sometimes cursed the fact that he lived for 89 years and wrote so much.'

With that strict set of criteria in mind, Chapman started to gather the material that would form the exhibition. Most of it, he knew, would be from the Museum's own extensive Michelangelo collection, but in order to tell the story he wanted to tell, he knew that he would have to borrow from other museums.

'It all began in 2000 when I went to the Teyler Museum in Haarlem, outside Amsterdam,' says Chapman. 'I'd been asked to write a review of their exhibition of Italian drawings, and it struck me that their Michelangelo drawings made a wonderful complement to what we have at the BM. I thought it would be wonderful to bring the two collections together, so I rather idly sent an e-mail to my opposite number at the Teyler. He said, "Yes, good idea – and I think you should do it because it was your idea." Once I got the green light from the British Museum, it became clear that it was going to be a bigger show than I envisaged, so I would need to borrow some more works. I approached the Ashmolean in Oxford and borrowed their very good group of Michelangelo drawings.'

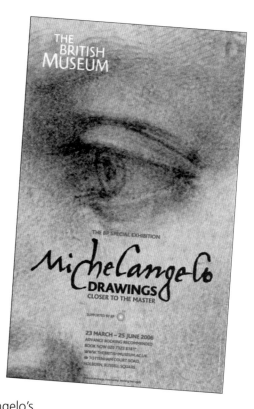

Above and overleaf: The *Michelangelo Drawings: Closer to the Master* exhibition of 2006 was one of the Museum's biggest successes, attracting 175,000 visitors.

Previous page: Michelangelo's
black chalk drawing of *The
Risen Christ*.

With his basic selection of over 100 drawings in mind, Chapman then set
about what he describes as 'the lonely part of the job' – writing the catalogue
that determines the structure of the exhibition, interprets the works and serves
as a souvenir, albeit a highly academic one. 'I was working till about 3 a.m. every
night, seven days a week. My family really came to hate Michelangelo during that
period. There were a few trips to the Teyler and the Ashmolean to see the
drawings, but for the most part I was either at a desk in the Prints and Drawings
department with my laptop or at home burning the midnight oil. Once the
book was written, the fun began. Actually putting the exhibition together is a
very collaborative process, and it's much more enjoyable.'

With his ideas still fresh in his mind, Chapman started working closely with
a team of designers and interpreters to make sure that the physical environment
and the written texts maximized the impact of the drawings. 'The design was
one of the main contributory factors to the success of the exhibition. You know
you'll sell tickets with Michelangelo – he's one of the names that guarantees
sales – but everyone agreed that the design made it really stunning. We agreed
right from the start that we wanted it to feel very fresh; that the drawings
should be easy to look at and there should be a high level of ambient lighting.
Often you go into art exhibitions and it's so dark and gloomy you have to strain
to look at the pictures, and you end up with a headache after half an hour. We
wanted to give people much clearer access to the drawings and to make it a
pleasant environment to be in.

'Beyond that, though, the design has a big influence on the way people
read the exhibition. Because I was working on a biographical theme, I wanted
to take people right through Michelangelo's career and to finish up with what I

*... the design has a big
influence on how people
read the exhibition*

consider to be the most extraordinary pieces in the show,
the three big Crucifixion drawings. The designers isolated
those in the last room, which was darker and more
sombre. It had enormous impact. We used texts from
Michelangelo's poetry on the walls and had the three
drawings beautifully lit. You got a strong sense of the
artist struggling with his own sense of mortality, his obsession with sin and
with the Cross as a symbol of redemption. That room worked well in terms of
humanizing Michelangelo, of showing him not just as a great artist but also
as a man terrified of death and desperately hoping for salvation. You'd come
through his whole career, the wonderful exuberance of his youthful figure
studies, the eroticism of his male nudes, and finally you were confronted with the
real man behind all the masks.'

3
Preparing objects for use

The care and preservation of the collection has always been at the top of the British Museum's list of priorities. But ideas about how best to do that, and how to put science and technology at the service of scholars and public, have changed dramatically in the last three centuries. 'If you look back beyond 100 years, the term "conservation" just wouldn't apply,' says David Saunders, head of the Conservation, Documentation and Science department. 'They thought much more in terms of restoration, of bringing ancient pieces into line with current taste. In the eighteenth and nineteenth centuries they'd take fragments of statues and put them together with a lot of plaster of Paris and other materials to try and replicate the whole original. In the twentieth century the pendulum swung the other way, towards a very purist approach of showing pieces only as archaeology. Sometimes that could be quite misguided because fragments in isolation can be very hard to understand. Now I think we're reaching a synthesis, where we present things in a way that shows the original intention but doesn't actually interfere with the integrity of the objects.'

The people in Conservation, Documentation and Science work across all the other departments, developing a range of skills and analytical techniques that can be applied to objects of every description. Conservation is concerned with the protection and preservation of objects, extending their lives for future generations. Documentation is an ongoing process of cataloguing the collection and making that information available to the widest-possible public; at present, the main project concerns getting the Museum catalogue online. Science develops new ways of looking at the collection, analysing materials and developing strategies for display, storage and conservation.

'Unlike the rest of the Museum, Conservation and Science are organized along material lines,' says Saunders, 'because the challenges that we face are more to do with physical substances rather than geographical or historical provenance. In Conservation, for instance, we're divided into stone, other inorganics, such as ceramics, glass and metal, pictorial art, which is mostly works on paper and silk, and organics, which includes wood, leather, ivory and textiles. It's useful to have that contrast with the way the rest of the Museum is organized because we start to see similarities and contrasts across a wide range of collections.'

Conservator Bridget Leach and curator Richard Parkinson examine a fragmentary Middle Kingdom papyrus from Egypt using a wide-screen microscope in the paper conservation studio.

Methods of conservation have changed almost as much as the ideas informing them. With each scientific advance, new methods are developed that enable the Museum's conservators to leave the lightest possible trace on the objects on which they are working. 'One of the buzz-words in conservation is reversibility,' says Saunders. 'In other words, is what I'm doing now going to affect the object for the rest of time, or will future generations be able to get back to how the object originally was before I got my hands on it? The nightmare for conservators is that something they do will alter the nature of the object or, even worse, damage it. Soluble nylon is a case in point: it was thought to be a sort of wonder substance a few years ago because it consolidated the surface of old wall paintings but was totally invisible. However, it's turned out to be a curse for all sorts of reasons. Firstly, it's not really "soluble" at all, and it's very difficult to get off once it's on. We could live with that, except for the fact that we've discovered that soluble nylon actually starts to change dimension after a few years. It shrinks and pulls off layers of paint. So with each new treatment that we develop, we have to ask ourselves whether what we're doing now is going to cause problems for the future. We try to analyse substances with accelerated ageing techniques, to find out what they will look like in five, ten, 20 years' time.'

> ... we have to ask ourselves whether what we're doing now is going to cause problems for the future

The focus in conservation is now, in Saunders's words, on 'preparing objects for use'. That's use in the widest-possible sense: putting them in an exhibition, sending them on the road for a museum loan, preparing them for photography or study, or just making sure that they're fit to be looked at as and when needed.

'Basically, it's any event that requires an object to be seen, handled or moved. Most of our work is driven by that need – so if something is just going to stay in a cupboard where it won't deteriorate, we won't touch it. If something is in danger of being lost, obviously it becomes a top priority; other than that, we respond to demand across all the collections. There are a lot of objects that we'd love to get our hands on and bring up to exhibition standards, but we have neither the time nor the money to do so. Those we survey carefully to make sure they don't slip into the "action" category. We keep an eye on storage conditions and keep deterioration to a minimum. Obviously everything deteriorates over time, but it doesn't have to be kept shiny and new looking. Some things are more volatile than others. A stone statue won't change much

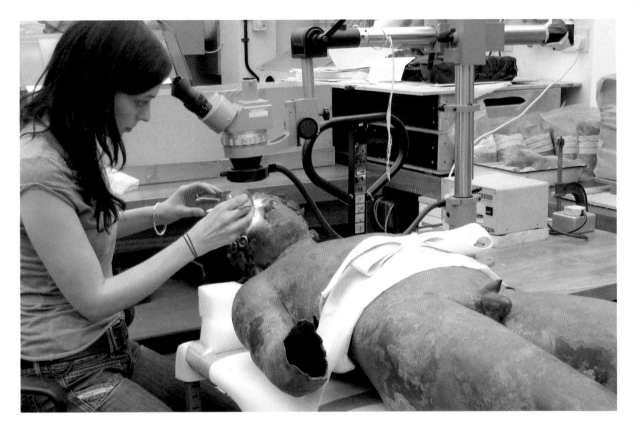

Above: Alexandra Baldwin gets to work on 'Charlie', the Roman statue of a youth, revealing concealed inlays on his eyes and lips.
Opposite: Installing the statue for exhibition. Now carefully conserved, he's a star of the Museum's collection.

in 100 years, whereas objects made of fur and feathers are deteriorating all the time, even if they're not used.'

A good example of the changing attitudes to conservation is the bronze statue of a youth from Ziphteh in the Nile Delta, a first-century BC sculpture made by Roman craftsmen in imitation of a Greek original. The youth – or 'Charlie' as he's known in the Museum – was discovered by Arab traders in the mid-nineteenth century and came to the Museum minus his legs, which had been melted down for reuse. Prior to purchase by the Museum he had been fully restored – his interior was filled with plaster and an internal iron armature supported the arms, which had become detached. In this way, he stood as a complete figure – but damage was being done.

'The plaster held a lot of moisture, which made the iron armature rust,' says Alexandra Baldwin, the BM conservator who is restoring Charlie to exhibition standard. 'When iron rusts it expands, so cracks had started appearing in the arms. Charlie went into the Conservation department for a long time in the 1960s and had all that Victorian restoration removed – he was there for so long that they gave him his nickname. For the last few years he's been tucked away in an upstairs gallery, but now we want to put him in a more prominent position, in a gallery between the Rosetta stone and the Elgin marbles. He's an important piece, the only large Roman bronze figure we have, and he deserves to be seen.'

Baldwin has been cleaning Charlie with a small scalpel, at 20 to 40 times magnification, removing loose corrosion and paint. 'When he was restored in the nineteenth century, he was painted black all over; that was the taste of the time. There are still bits of black paint on him, especially under his arms and round his back. We're getting back to a nice, overall surface that shows the quality of the bronze, which would originally have looked like tanned skin. There are some inlays as well: we've discovered that the eyes are inlaid with silver, and the lips and nipples are inlaid with copper, to give a pink tone. By getting down to this level, we can see toolmarks and evidence of where the separate casts were riveted together, which can tell us about how he was made and assembled.'

The newly spruced-up Charlie went back on display at the beginning of 2007 and looks set to be one of the new stars of the collection. 'It used to be thought that he represented the god Apollo,' says Baldwin, 'because of the topknot on his head. But now we think he was something much more humble, possibly a decorative lamp-holder. There are remains of fittings in his hands,

ALEXANDRA
BALDWIN

Conservator

I'M WHAT'S CALLED AN 'INORGANICS CONSERVATOR', which means I work with glass, ceramics and metal across the whole of the Museum's collection. But my particular speciality is metal, and I have a particular attachment to the Greek and Roman department – I'm their representative in the metal-conservation section. As well as working on the Roman bronze known as 'Charlie', I've been working on the collection of Greek and Roman lead objects that comprises about 2000 things, from pipes and seals to children's toys and votive offerings. I like the lead objects – they're not very glamorous, but they were once in everyone's home. Lead is obviously very malleable and often highly decorated – it was the plastic of its day as it was cheap and easily formed, so it was used for a great variety of things. Not everyone had a nice gold brooch, but you can bet they had a few bits of lead.

I got interested in archaeology when I was quite young, and used to volunteer on digs near my home in Chichester in West Sussex. Since coming to the British Museum in 2002, I've been to excavation sites near Rome, which is a real thrill. It's great to be there with all the other experts and to see things coming fresh off the dig. In the Museum the conservators are in a separate building from the curators, so you're at one remove from them – but on a dig you're often all in the same room, sharing your knowledge and your skills.

I don't just work on the Greek and Roman material; one of the nice things about being a conservator is that you get your hands on so many different things. I've worked on objects from the Tell es-Sa'idiyeh excavations in Jordan, and from the Sutton Hoo burial, and on some Japanese fifth-century horse harnesses – so there's plenty of variety!

where you could have hung ceramic or metal oil lamps. Charlie was probably one of a pair that stood on either side of a doorway. I know it's a bit of a comedown from Apollo, but I actually like the fact that he's quite a domestic figure. It makes him more approachable.'

British Museum scientists work hand in hand with the Conservation department from their laboratories in Russell Square. 'The Science department has two major roles,' says Saunders. 'Firstly, they're here to answer questions about objects from a curatorial point of view: what are they made of, when were they made, how were they made, where did the materials come from? Secondly, they provide methods for the conservation of objects. A conservator might want to get something off the surface of an object, or join two pieces together safely; often they'll know how to do it already, but sometimes they need a scientist to look at the materials and see how they might interact. And, of course, we're always looking at ways of slowing down the deterioration process, analysing the effects of light, humidity, pollution and pests. Every object in the collection is subject to those three lines of inquiry: curatorial, conservatorial and scientific.'

Like conservators, scientists try to analyse objects without altering them in any way. 'The best form of analysis is the one that doesn't even touch the object,' says Saunders. 'You can do a great deal with hand lenses and microscopes: you can spot structures and materials, you can spot crystal forms, particles and so on. After that we have non-invasive techniques that don't require taking a sample, such as X-ray fluorescence, which fires a beam of X-rays at the surface of an object in order to analyse the different elements in compounds. Spectroscopy can also give compound-specific information on the chemical make-up of materials.

> The best form of analysis is one that doesn't touch the object

'If we can take a sample from an object without damaging it in any way, it can go under a scanning electron microscope, which is one of the most powerful analytical methods we have – it can tell us about how layers are built up, what they're made of. If we're working on a wall painting, for instance, we can build up a picture of exactly how it was painted, what the materials were and in what order they went on. But we'd only ever take a sample from the edge of existing damage, around a crack or somewhere that the paint is crumbling. We only need a sample the size of a pinhead; it's not like we're snapping off a couple of centimetres!'

Scientific analysis can tell us a huge amount about objects that seem, at first glance, to be shrouded in mystery. Take, for instance, the double-headed serpent in the Mexican Gallery. It's a beautiful object, carved in wood and covered with turquoise mosaic, and one of the most popular in the Museum's collection – but nobody really knows why it was made or what it was used for. It may have been worn as a chest ornament during ceremonial occasions by Aztec priests. It could have been held up on a standard or used as a temple decoration. Basically, however, its function remains a mystery.

But scientific analysis can tell us a great deal about the people who made it. Materials scientist Caroline Cartwright has worked on the mosaics for over ten years and has discovered a huge wealth of information about their creation.

'My entry point is the wood,' she says. 'That's my area of specialist expertise. Most of the turquoise mosaics are built on intricately carved wood, so we have to go back to that material when we start our investigation. I can identify the wood by looking at it under a high-powered optical microscope; each tree has a very distinctive cellular pattern that you learn to recognize with experience. In this case, the wood the Aztec/Mixtec carpenters used is *Cedrela odorata*, part of the mahogany family that was quite widespread in Mexico in the sixteenth century, when these objects were probably made. It's quite a dense wood, but easily carved, so the craftsmen certainly picked the right material to work with. It's aromatic, which may have been important if this were an object to be used in religious or ceremonial rituals. It's insect-resistant too, which has helped all these objects to last so well.

'From the wood, my attention turns to the shell that's used on the head and for the gums and teeth. Again, you can tell exactly what it is by looking at it in the scanning electron microscope, and here they've used a variety of materials. The bright white teeth are made of queen conch, *Strombus gigas*, a very strong material. The coloured inserts are made from thorny oyster, *Spondylus princeps*, which comes in quite a variety of shades. They've used the bright reds and oranges on the front, the paler pink and yellows for the back.

Below and opposite: The double-headed serpent is one of the iconic items in the British Museum's collection. The front (below) is covered in a complex pattern of turquoise and shell; the reverse (opposite) reveals the skilfully carved wooden base.

'Then there's the turquoise itself, which again comes in a variety of colours and allows the artists to give additional modelling to the serpent. We think that it came from the southwestern United States, but we're currently doing a follow-up project to find out if there were any local sources in Mexico. There's also mother-of-pearl, which would have come from quite far afield, and some specialized resin to hold everything in place.'

So what does all this information really tell us, other than the fact that these were clever craftsmen with a range of materials at their disposal? 'What we're seeing here is a number of different skills involved in the making of a single object,' says Cartwright. 'It's very unlikely that one person would have made a double-headed serpent by themselves. I think it would go to different workshops for a variety of specialists to work on it: a wood-carver, a worker in shell, a lapidary for the turquoise and so on. It's opened our eyes to the way that Aztec or Mixtec society may have worked, and it suggests that this was a society supporting many highly skilled craftsmen working with very valuable materials.

'Also, it tells us much about the trading practices of the Aztec people. They've sourced materials from quite a wide geographical area, so they must

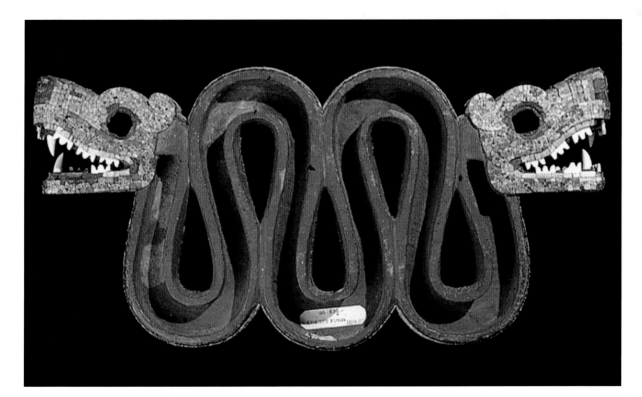

CAROLINE CARTWRIGHT

Materials Scientist

MY JOB IS PRINCIPALLY TO IDENTIFY WOOD and other plant remains from objects across all the departments. I trained as an archaeologist and a botanist, so it's the perfect job for me – and I like the fact that I cross all cultural, geographical and time boundaries. I can be working simultaneously on objects from Oceania, Ancient Egypt and Mexico, for example, and it's quite a different way of looking at the collection.

There's quite a strong element of fieldwork to my job; I'm not in a laboratory all the time. I do some work on British sites, but usually I'm called out to go somewhere hot, such as sites in Jordan, for example the excavations at Tell es-Sa'idiyeh, which is a palace complex and burial ground. There I carry out on-site sampling to find out the range of organic materials. As well as managing my team of specialists on the excavation, I give some guidance to the workmen, telling them what to look out for. Charcoal, for instance, can give us much information. From its anatomical structure I can tell what sort of tree it came from, whether it was wood that was burnt in an accidental fire or whether it had been made into charcoal for fuel. To an untrained eye it might just be a bit of old charcoal, but to archaeologists it says a great deal about how the people lived and what their surrounding environment was like.

Wood can tell you so much about the culture and people that made the object. Egyptian mummy cases, for instance, are made out of certain sorts of wood that are favourable to the preservation of bodies and will last for a long time; that tells us that the ancient Egyptians had a sophisticated understanding of their materials. Recently I've been working on some of the Roman period Egyptian mummy portraits (see left), for which the carpenters largely rejected the use of local timbers in favour of the higher-quality linden wood from Europe. That was a very exciting discovery that nobody had known about before I looked at thin sections of wood from those portraits under a high-powered optical microscope and identified the wood from its anatomical structure. So now we know the full extent of the Egyptian trade sources and compelling cultural influences in this period, which extended into Europe. Oak, also from Europe, is occasionally used for those portraits, as is sycamore fig (*Ficus sycomorus*), which is a local wood, but neither of them holds the paint so well on the wood's prepared surface as linden, which the artists obviously understood.

have established regular trading relationships way beyond their immediate vicinity. It's a measure of their sophistication as a culture, and that's hard to get from other sources. The written and painted records can only tell us so much, but when you start analysing an object like the serpent it gives a lot more information. Of course, it raises far more questions than it can ever answer, but I like that. Wouldn't it be boring if we knew all the answers and we could just put the object back in its box or showcase? To me, that would mean that the object was dead.'

> **If we knew all the answers ... To me that would mean that the object was dead**

One of the biggest conservation projects in the British Museum in recent years has focused on a series of ancient Egyptian wall paintings from the tomb-chapel of Nebamun, a grain accountant in fourteenth-century BC Thebes. These 11 fragments, regarded as some of the finest artistic products of the ancient world, are among the treasures of the British Museum. They tell us a huge amount about the way in which people lived in Egypt in the late eighteenth dynasty (about 1350 BC). The paintings were acquired in 1821,

Below: One of the fragments of the banqueting scene from the painted tomb-chapel of Nebamun from around 1350 BC.

KAREN BIRKHÖLZER

Conservator

THE BULK OF MY WORKING LIFE for the last few years has been the Nebamun project. Sometimes the job can get monotonous; you'll be working for months and months just staring down a microscope, laying down flakes of loose paint, which is very routine work indeed. But then suddenly you find yourself looking at something and it just grabs you. The paintings are full of surprises, and I'm still discovering new things even after five years. For me, *Fowling in the Marshes* is the most beautiful of them. It's so intensely alive, and I'm still surprised by it. The painting of the cat's eye, for instance, is something that I can never get bored of.

I've been at the British Museum since 1993. I'm from Berlin originally, and when I left school I didn't really know what I wanted to do, but I was quite certain that it had to be something that had a practical element to it. I didn't know what conservation was at the time – most people didn't – it wasn't the professionalized discipline that it's become today. I studied art history in Berlin and Cologne, then did an internship in easel-painting conservation before coming to London to study sculpture conservation at the City & Guilds of London Art School. It was hard work, very intensive, and it led to an internship at the British Museum. I've been here ever since.

Conservators are very committed people; we have a deep love for what we do. That's not something that I'd admit all the time because, like everyone else, we sometimes get fed up with our jobs or frustrated with a project. But I know that I'm really lucky to be working on something that I love doing. I spend my day working on the most beautiful, most important artefacts in the world. How many people can say that?

taken from a tomb-chapel somewhere in Thebes, and they were on continuous display at the Museum from 1835 until 1997.

The paintings had to be removed from public display because of gallery refurbishment and building works in preparation for the redevelopment of the Great Court, and this gave the chance to conserve and analyse them fully. There were other reasons for working on the Nebamun paintings. 'In a temporary exhibition in 1999, we placed two fragments side by side, as closely as possible,' says Egyptologist Richard Parkinson. 'It worked so well that we commissioned a full-scale remounting of the paintings, not just to conserve them, but so that we can display them as parts of a single, continuous, painted wall.'

To understand the conservation of the Nebamun wall paintings, it's necessary to go back to the mysterious day in 1820 when they were first discovered. 'We know a great deal about the paintings in the ancient world, who they show and what they mean, but we know very little about how they were found in the nineteenth century,' says Parkinson. 'They were acquired for the British proconsul in Egypt, Henry Salt, one of the great benefactors of the Egyptian collectors here, by his agent Giovanni d'Athanasi, somewhere in Luxor. But we don't know exactly where the tomb was, we don't know how big it was, or what the floor-plan looked like. There's no record. It must have been a very spectacular tomb, but it's just disappeared! Understanding the paintings is like doing a jigsaw puzzle where you have only 10 per cent of the pieces. But I managed to join two of the fragments together, which was a huge thrill.'

What we do know is that d'Athanasi was selective in the fragments that he acquired for Salt. 'Everything he got has fluffy animals or naked girls or great piles of food on it – so it seems that d'Athanasi was deliberately targeting the English taste! We know that the paintings were in d'Athanasi's house in Luxor one afternoon in July 1821 because someone went in and drew them. We know that they were packed up and shipped to London, where they waited for ages in the Medway Estuary for an import licence. What we don't know is what happened in the weeks immediately before they arrived in d'Athanasi's house. We're still looking for clues, and maybe one day we'll find out exactly where they came from, but at the moment I don't hold out much hope.'

These are fragile pieces now, painted on a plaster skim laid over a mud backing. They were never meant to be moved. In an ideal world, perhaps, they would have stayed right there, in the underground tomb-chapel. That was not the way in the 1820s, however, and although we now frown on the brutal methods of early collectors like d'Athanasi, I suppose we do have to thank them for preserving works of art that might otherwise never have survived at all.

THE YAXCHILÁN LINTELS

The Yaxchilán lintels were carved in about AD 700 at the height of the Maya civilization in Mexico, and they used to be set above doorways in the temple at Yaxchilán. I went there once, when I was doing research into the conservation of Maya low-relief carvings – it's right in the middle of the jungle, and it's quite a trek to get there, but it's the most beautiful site. Working on them here at the Museum, and seeing the traces of paint on them, gives you a wonderful insight into what that temple site would once have looked like.

The lintels show the ritual of bloodletting that was an important part of Maya life, tied up with visionary experiences and ancestor worship. The woman shown here is Lady Wak Tuun, one of the wives of the ruler Bird Jaguar, and she's carrying a basket containing a rope and a stingray spine that she'll use to pierce various parts of her body in a ritual. The creature springing up before her is a cross between a serpent and an ancestor, and it's going to take her into the land of ancestral spirits.

KAREN BIRKHÖLZER, *Conservator*

Above: Karen Birkhölzer and Richard Parkinson inspect conservation work on the *Fowling in the Marshes* scene from the Nebamun tomb paintings.

So what are they, these fragments with a strange history on which so many of the British Museum's resources are being lavished? They were painted for the tomb-chapel of Nebamun, a grain accountant in the temple of Amun in Luxor, around the reign of Amenhotep III (1390–1352 BC). They depict scenes of elite daily life – banquets, agriculture, animal husbandry, hunting and religious offerings. Much of the iconography is common to other tomb paintings of the

MY FATHER WAS AN ARTIST, and the house was always full of art books, so that's how I first became interested in Ancient Egypt. I remember looking at the paintings in those books, including the Nebamun tomb paintings, and being very fascinated by them. I particularly loved the script, so I taught myself to read hieroglyphs a bit; it's really quite an easy script. When I went to Oxford, I chose Egyptology over English literature because it's easier to read English literature on your own and find your own way, whereas for Egyptian literature you really need some specialist training!

I became very interested in the poetry of Ancient Egypt, and there were certain poems that I wanted to be able to read in the original. One always has to go back to the source whenever possible; translations of poetry are very useful, but they're not the real thing. I'm actually terrible at spoken languages, but Ancient Egyptian is a nice dead language, and I don't have to speak it. If there are vowels, I just can't cope.

At the moment my main research project, apart from Nebamun, is on a major collection of papyri discovered by the famous British archaeologist Flinders Petrie in the 1890s. It's a priest's library, including a lot of magic spells, but it also contained written copies of two of the great poems of the Middle Kingdom, *The Tale of Sinuhe* and *The Tale of the Eloquent Peasant*, written around 1850 BC. They're wonderful masterpieces of world literature, wild and passionate poems, and they're the things that really got me interested in Egyptology in the first place. Whenever I can, I try to lecture about these poems – this year at Cologne, Oxford and Göttingen – partly for the beauty of the poetry, but also to show students the importance of the original papyri, and that poetry is, like everything, a material artefact from a particular culture.

To my horror, I recently discovered a note in the archives that revealed that the British Museum was offered the main manuscripts of *Sinuhe* and *The Eloquent Peasant* for about £70 in the 1840s, and we didn't buy them. They went to Berlin instead; their Egyptologists then were obviously more perceptive and had more money. It's a bit like having the only copies of Shakespeare, Milton and Jane Austen in a single library. I was very nearly physically sick when I found that memorandum. Fortunately, it's quite easy to get to Berlin these days, and we work closely with other museums.

I go to Egypt about twice a year, usually giving lectures on tours. I can't go on excavations, much as I'd like to, because I'm diabetic, and I know from experience that my health can't stand the rigours of fieldwork very well. Fortunately for me, Egyptology is not just about excavations, it's also about investigating what we already have and the beauty of the Museum's paintings and poetic papyri is absolutely inexhaustible.

RICHARD PARKINSON

Curator specializing in Ancient Egyptian Culture

Above: *Fowling in the Marshes*. Nebamun stands on a papyrus boat, with his wife Hatshepsut behind him and his daughter below. The scene would have been balanced by another of Nebamun spearing fish; the tip of his spear is just visible at the bottom left-hand side of the picture.

period, evoking the dead man's hopes for the afterlife. But that's where the similarity between these and other tomb paintings ends.

'There's an argument for regarding this as one of the greatest artistic achievements of the ancient Egyptian world,' says Richard Parkinson. 'Other tomb painters of the period portray similar scenes but with nothing like the same energy and creativity. Take the most famous fragment, the scene of Nebamun fowling in the marshes. It's a standard image of the tomb owner standing on a little skiff in the marshes catching birds, and you see it in a lot of other tomb paintings. It's about imposing order on nature, catching food and having fun in the afterlife. Other artists show elegant figures against a background of vertical papyrus clumps. But the Nebamun artist's work is exploding with life and detail. The papyrus twists outwards, bursting towards Nebamun. The picture isn't just full of birds: it's crammed with animals of all sorts, fish, insects and, of course, a cat. Wherever there's an empty space, he's put a butterfly. Lotus flowers are springing up all around the boat. The figure of Nebamun himself is very masculine, and his wife is very feminine – much more curvaceous and full than many portrayals of women from this period. The details are astonishing: we can identify every species of bird and fish. As for the cat, it's full of character; it's slightly wild and trying to leap on to the birds. It even has a gilded eye, which we've seen nowhere else in tomb paintings of this period. We probably have to thank the cat for the survival of this fragment because d'Athanasi knew that Henry Salt would like it. The other half of the composition is lost. Some fragments were seen on the art market in Cairo in the 1940s, but they've disappeared.'

Why would a simple grain accountant end up with such a spectacular tomb? 'Many people in the Luxor area would have been paid through the temple granaries, so even though Nebamun's job sounds quite lowly, he was actually a man of considerable indirect influence. He could decide whether people got paid or not. He's not a VIP as such, not a high priest or a vizier, but a man of great practical importance, who could call in favours when he needed them. I can imagine him sidling up to one of the finest painters in the land, saying, "Perhaps you could spend a fortnight painting a nice little tomb for me?" His tomb is small, the paintings were done quickly, and they probably weren't so expensive, but he obviously got the right man for the job!' We can only imagine what the bigger, grander tomb-chapel

OSTRACON OF THE TALE OF SINUHE

I've done a great deal of work on the Rosetta stone – one of the most wonderful objects in the Museum – but it isn't my favourite! It's not very beautiful, though it's important because it came to Europe at the right time and triggered the process of decipherment. It doesn't really matter what it looks like; it's the concept that counts, and it represents the triumph of ideas, which is, I think, why it fascinates so many people.

My favourite object is actually an ugly, little ostracon that, of course, we couldn't read without the Rosetta stone. It's a flake of limestone that was used by ancient Egyptian scribes for writing on, with a copy of the final stanza of The Tale of Sinuhe *on it. It was written by an apprentice scribe in about 1200 BC, and it contains a few spelling mistakes and reinterpretations of the text. You can see that he was learning his craft. I like the humanity of that. It was already a very old poem when he was copying it out, and it shows how we are always simultaneously re-creating and garbling the past. If we make mistakes in the twenty-first century, we're certainly not the first to do so.*

The ostracon combines great poetry, which talks about human emotions, with a real sense of human effort and fallibility. It tells us a lot about ancient cultures and a lot about ourselves.

RICHARD PARKINSON, *Curator specializing in Ancient Egyptian Culture*

Above: Musicians and dancers entertain the guests at a banquet depicted in Nebamun's tomb. The face-on representation of the musicians is very rare in Egyptian art.

paintings of the area were like. Amenhotep III was like the Sun King of ancient Egypt, the wealthiest pharaoh of all; Tutankhamun, by comparison, was the poor relation. If a small, insignificant bureaucrat like Nebamun had a tomb-chapel this good, then the big men's stuff must have been incredible.

The six-year conservation work on the paintings is a long project – much longer than usual, but there was much work to be done. Karen Birkhölzer is one of the conservators who has been working on the Nebamun paintings ever since they arrived in the Conservation department, and she knows better than anyone the painstaking processes that will preserve these works for posterity.

'The paintings are being conserved from top to bottom, from the painted surface right through to the mud backing,' she says. 'Where necessary, they're being remounted. The pictures have been through a lot: they were cut off the walls of the tomb, shipped to England, mounted in plaster, shipped off to a quarry during the Second World War and displayed on the walls of a public gallery for the rest of the time. With all that treatment and travel, they weren't in the best of shape.

'The main problem was the plaster-of-Paris backing, which had started compressing the paintings. It was flush with the surface of the paintings, so we've taken it back by at least 5 mm to expose the mud. We have to remove it carefully bit by bit with a scalpel, and it's a hard job because there's nowhere to rest your hands. Eventually we'll put a skim over the surface to cover the remaining plaster, which will be painted to gallery colour so that the eye will be drawn to the painting, not to the glaring-white plaster of Paris.

'Some of the paintings will be completely remounted in new frames. For instance, there are two fragments showing a banqueting scene, which were mounted separately – but we've now shown that they are both part of the same scene, and they are separated by the exact distance of a saw cut. We're putting them back together again for the first time since they came off the tomb wall.'

Below: Karen working on the paintings.

Before that big, heavy work is done, the conservators have to focus their attention on the delicate, painted surface. 'We've gone over the whole surface of every painting, millimetre by millimetre, laying down every loose and dis-lodged flake of paint,' says Birkhölzer. 'We're using a technique developed in this museum, in which an acrylic adhesive with a wetting agent is applied to the surface. As the water evaporates, it pulls down the flake and secures it. Then we go over the surface with acetone, where necessary, to remove any residue or shine. Once it's set, it's set, and the surface isn't tarnished in any way. It's a nerve-racking process. When I look through a microscope at the surface of the painting, I see a little piece of paint that's finer than a hair. And I have to touch that with my tiny little brush, with a blob of adhesive on the end that looks absolutely massive. If I catch the flake on my brush, I risk pulling it off altogether. But I've got the hang of it, and it works very well. It's very satisfying.'

> We've gone over the whole surface of every painting, millimetre by millimetre …

Because of the nature of the fragments, hollows have developed between the mud backing and the gypsum surface, which means that, displayed upright, the paintings could literally start dropping out of their frames. 'You can tell when something is hollow quite easily,' says Birkhölzer, 'just by giving it a light tap with your fingernail. If it's solid, it hardly makes any sound. If it's hollow, the sound is deeper and louder. Once you know you have hollow areas, you can't apply any sort of pressure to the surface because they might just crumble.

And the paintings can't be displayed vertically; they have to be at an angle to prevent gravity from pulling off those hollow bits.'

One of the biggest questions in all art conservation concerns pigments. The Nebamun paintings were created with a fairly limited palette of earth colours, applied with small brushstrokes to give a maximum range of colours. Blue and green frits (pigments made of crushed glass in a resin-binding medium) were added to the palette, and there were highlights in gold. The earth colours are stable, but the frits have largely gone.

'Frit is a very unstable pigment. The binding medium shrinks in time, and the grains of coloured glass simply drop out. You can tell where it used to be on the painting because the binder leaves a trace; most of it is in the collars and necklaces or on leaves. We won't be replacing those colours on the paintings; that would be restoration rather than conservation.'

There are great plans for the newly conserved fragments. When they're finished they'll be shown in a purpose-built gallery that will seek to re-create the impact they would have had in their original tomb-chapel setting.

'When we read ancient written accounts of tomb paintings, we see words like "entertainment" and "beauty",' says Richard Parkinson. 'We'd like to get modern visitors to respond in the same way. The problem with Egyptian art is that we often assume it's something weird and primitive, that at best it is just decoration with a liturgical or magical function. I want to reclaim these works as art, not just bits of plaster painted with strange gods. Of course the content is religious, in the same way that Michelangelo's Sistine Chapel paintings are religious, but there's another set of values that's all about visual wonder and pleasure. That's why we are going to try to present the paintings in the same order and position as they might have been displayed in the tomb-chapel. I want people to walk into the room and have the visceral experience of being confronted with great, exuberant works of art.'

> I want to reclaim these works as art, not just bits of plaster painted with strange gods

4

A place full of treasure

A place full of treasure

A quick glance around any of the galleries in the British Museum is enough to convince most people that the place is full of treasure. But the word 'treasure', which can be used generally to describe anything of great value or beauty, is fraught with complicated meanings, both legal and academic, that direct a great deal of curatorial activity within the BM. In its academic sense, 'treasure' could mean almost any object that contributes significantly to the understanding of a certain culture. Take the Vindolanda tablets, for instance, a collection of handwritten documents on wood from the late first or early second century AD, from the Roman fort of Vindolanda (modern Chesterholm) in Northumberland. In basic terms, they're just bits of decaying wood with some scribbles on them – but to a historian they're beyond price, telling us more about Roman Britain than any amount of gold could ever hope to do.

Below: Gareth Williams, curator of early medieval coinage.

And yet despite their academic and cultural value, those fragile, written records do not count as treasure in the legal sense. Since coming into effect in 1997, the Treasure Act 1996, which applies to England, Wales and Northern Ireland, has placed a very specific definition on exactly what constitutes treasure, and what has to happen to it when it is discovered. (Scotland has a different law that covers all ancient objects, regardless of what they are made of. In the Scottish Law of Treasure Trove, the Crown can claim any finds of any objects of any date where the original owner cannot be traced.) Administered by the BM in England, the National Museums & Galleries of Wales and the Department for the Government for Northern Ireland, it's a piece of legislation designed to clarify the ownership of things that are discovered by members of the public, often using metal detectors, and also during excavations. So 'treasure' now falls into four main categories. Firstly, any object more than 300 years old when found, which is made of more than 10 per cent silver or gold. Secondly, at least two gold or silver coins from the same find, or ten or more of base metal (for example, copper-alloy), again provided they are at least 300 years old. Thirdly, more than two objects of prehistoric metalwork from the same find with less than 10 per cent gold or silver. And finally, any objects found in association with treasure, such as glass beads or vessels found in a grave with gold or silver items, or the pottery container of a coin hoard.

Above: The Vindolanda tablets, handwritten documents on wood from the late first or early second century AD. They were found in the remains of a Roman fort in Northumberland.

So much for the legal definitions – but what happens to the stuff once it's been found? Again, the Treasure Act has the answers, legally obliging the finders to report it to their local coroner within 14 days. If a museum is interested in acquiring the object, the coroner then holds an inquest to determine whether or not the find constitutes treasure (often following expert advice from the British Museum or the network of finds liaison officers of the Portable Antiquities Scheme (PAS), a programme of finds-recording for England, Wales and Northern Ireland). If it's not treasure, the owner can do with the object whatever he or she likes. If it is treasure, a whole new procedure comes into play. The find is the property of the Crown, which means that it is offered to a museum to acquire. The finder and landowner are eligible for a reward equivalent to the full market value of the find, which is set by an independent board of experts. Only if no museum expresses an interest in the item, or is unable to purchase it, can the finder retain it.

Take the case of the Winchester hoard, one of the most significant archaeological discoveries of the last 50 years, unearthed in 2000 by a metal detectorist in a field in Hampshire. The hoard comprises two sets of gold jewellery, made in the first century BC, each consisting of a necklace torc and two gold brooches. One set also had two bracelets. A total of 1160 g of very pure gold went into making these objects, which may have belonged to a married couple, as one torc is substantially bigger than the other.

Two of the brooches and one of the torcs were found by detectorist Kevan Halls, who recognized the significance of his discovery and immediately

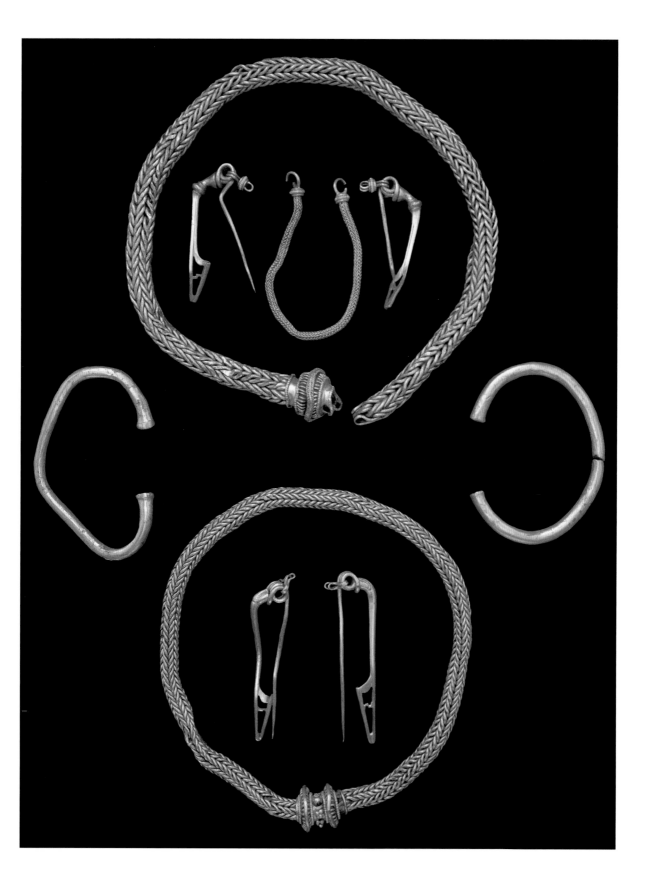

informed the PAS. They called in archaeologists from the British Museum, who quickly realized the magnitude of the find.

'When I took on my job, my predecessor told me that I'd get only one major treasure hoard in my career,' says J. D. Hill, curator of the British and European Iron Age collections. 'And the Winchester hoard came up within two years of me being here! When I first heard about what the detectorist had found, I just didn't believe it; I thought it had to be a hoax. But then we started doing fieldwork on the site. A second torc was found, then the rest of the hoard. The necklaces are utterly unique objects; there's nothing like them anywhere else in the world. They're very thick and massive, which is characteristic of British Iron Age jewellery, but they weren't made in northern Europe. The workmanship is Roman or Hellenistic; they must have been made by a craftsman in the Mediterranean, who either visited northern Europe or made them for someone from Britain, or they were made in the Mediterranean as a gift for someone in Britain. Roman jewellery is very fine and delicate; this has been scaled up to a massiveness that would appeal to "barbarian" tastes. Even back then, rich Brits had a taste for chunky gold jewellery.'

It took no time at all for the coroner to decide that the Winchester hoard was treasure, and it was offered to a museum. The British Museum had made the all-important expression of interest and set about raising the money. It was acquired (with the agreement of the local museum) with help from the National Heritage Memorial Fund, the National Art Collections Fund (now called the Art Fund) and the British Museum Friends.

'We acquired it,' says Hill, 'because of its tremendous historical importance. It tells us a great deal about life in pre-Roman Britain. This jewellery was made around the time that Julius Caesar was making his conquests in France and showing some interest in Britain – and it tells us that there were some very powerful people in the Hampshire area at the time, rich enough to commission this kind of work from a skilled Mediterranean craftsman. That knowledge changes our picture of what was going on in southern England. These were very powerful people – possibly a king and a queen – with whom the Romans would have had to be on good terms. These aren't grave goods, and they weren't found in architectural remains; they were buried as an offering.'

Like all treasure cases, the money that was paid by the British Museum was shared by the finder and landowner. Treasure objects belong, by legal

> ... its tremendous historical importance ... tells us a great deal about life in pre-Roman Britain

Opposite: The Winchester hoard dates from the first century BC. It was discovered in 2000 and is considered to be one of the most important archaeological discoveries of the last 50 years.

CITOLE

My absolute favourite is the citole, a carved musical instrument from the late thirteenth or early fourteenth century, a sort of medieval guitar. It was heavily modified in the sixteenth century, when it belonged either to Elizabeth I or to Robert Dudley, Earl of Leicester – there's a little metal plate bearing both coats of arms – and turned into something more closely resembling a violin, with a fingerboard, a bridge and so on. The carving is breathtakingly intricate and beautiful, full of fantastic animal and plant shapes, but it's also got a really interesting history. People think of the Middle Ages as a backward period, but when you see the beauty they were capable of creating, you realize it was anything but. As a musician myself, I appreciate a good musical instrument, and I've played the part of Robert Dudley in full costume, here in the Museum and elsewhere, so I feel a special affinity with the citole. If someone would produce a replica, I'd love to have a go.

GARETH WILLIAMS, *Curator of Early Medieval Coinage*

definition, to the Crown – but the person who finds them and the owner of the land on which they are found have the right to be rewarded the market value of the find. If a museum expresses interest in a treasure object and then manages to buy it at an officially agreed price, the museum pays that money to the government, which then disburses the same sum to the finder/landowner as a reward.

But what happens when something of great importance is discovered that is not protected by the Treasure Act? In theory, if something is not legally defined as treasure, the landowner or finder can dispose of it however they like – but this is where we enter a much more grey area in terms of value. When the Coenwulf coin was found by a metal detectorist in Bedfordshire in 2001, it was instantly clear to experts that this was a unique and important item, a gold 'mancus' from the late eighth or early ninth century struck for Coenwulf, King of Mercia. It tells us much about the history, politics and trade of that period, and it's extremely well preserved. But is it treasure? Not according to the Act, which states that only two or more gold or silver coins found together can be legally defined as such. The Coenwulf coin, then, for all its monetary and historical value, fell outside the remit of the Treasure Act, leaving it at the mercy of market forces. Thus began a turbulent process that led, happily, to the BM's acquisition of the coin in 2006 – by the skin of its teeth. Gareth Williams, curator of Early Medieval Coinage, supervised the project from the word go.

'The whole process was hair-raising,' he says, 'and we very nearly lost the coin on several occasions. There were so many complications. First of all, the detectorist who found the coin was under the misconception that common land has no owner and therefore hadn't sought the landowner's permission to detect on that site. He wanted to sell it directly to us, but it turned out that he didn't have the right to because he wasn't the legal owner of the coin. Then we discovered that particular patch of land was the subject of a legal dispute

ONE OF THE CHALLENGES of working in the Museum is addressing a wide variety of audiences. The people who come here have a lot of different levels of knowledge, and we have to address them all – and I think that's good for the curators as well as the public. It encourages communication. There's a tendency for scholars to become inward looking, only addressing their academic peers or graduates and undergraduates. Here we have the same academic standards as a university, but we're also addressing primary-school children, the general public of all ages, enthusiastic amateurs and overseas visitors. We can't just write learned articles in impenetrable prose. We need to get complicated ideas across in simple words, that's good for us and it's a great challenge.

We're developing new ways of communicating with people. One thing I'm keen on is costume and enactment; it really seems to break down barriers. We had a finds day at the Museum recently, where people were bringing all sorts of objects, and we needed to give them some clue as to who to talk to. I started the day dressed as a Tudor gentleman so that people knew they could talk to me about that period. Later I joined the Vikings for a battle on the front lawn. Costume is great fun, but it has a practical application as well. Part of my Tudor outfit was a sword belt with metal sliders – they're like buckles that slide up and down to adjust the length of the straps that hold the scabbard. A man came up to me, a metal detectorist, and said, 'Aha! I find things that look just like that all the time. Now I know what they are.'

I belong to a Viking enactment group based in Leicester and we do shows around the Midlands and elsewhere. It takes quite a lot of time and money, but I learn a hell of a lot from it for a research project I'm doing on Viking warfare. I got involved when the group was doing an enactment at a castle near where I live, and I got talking to the chap who ran it. I was impressed by what they were doing, and he was interested in my research, so we decided to work together. There's a lot of scope for practical experimentation, to see how certain weapons or items of clothing and kit actually worked. We make nearly all our own stuff: we have a practising black-smith who does the serious metalwork, and we can all make costumes. Obviously the weapons are modified; we're not actually trying to kill each other.

A few years ago, professional archaeologists laughed at enactment groups, but now there's a shift in attitude, just as there has been towards metal detectorists. We have to appreciate their contribution, and we should be working with them rather than against them. Metal detectorists are being embraced far more by the museums community, and the line between enactment and experimental archaeology is also being blurred. We're not just silly people dressing up for fun; we're seriously investigating the skills, methods and equipment used by these cultures.

We use re-enactors quite a lot in the Museum now, particularly Romans, Anglo-Saxons and Vikings. The public enjoys it and engages with it. When I first started there was a certain amount of laughter among my colleagues, and in some cases an attitude that curators just shouldn't do that sort of thing. But as an institution, we've moved on. Enactment is seen as a useful tool for research and for extending access to the collection, and my experience in that field is seen as a positive asset.

GARETH WILLIAMS

Curator of Early Medieval Coinage

Right: The Coenwulf coin, found by a metal detectorist in Bedfordshire in 2001 and acquired by the British Museum in 2006 – but only just!

anyway, so we had to wait for a long time to find out who had the legal right to sell the coin. Once that was resolved, the owners had to decide what they wanted to do; remember, they were under absolutely no legal obligation to offer the coin to a museum, as it's not legally treasure.

'The legal owners decided not to sell the coin directly to us, but to put it up for auction. We bid, but not successfully, and the coin was bought by an American dealer with a British partner, who put it up for an export licence in order to be able to sell it on in the States. That's when we thought we'd lost it for good. But the government delayed the export licence to give a museum in this country the chance to buy the coin. After a lot of wrangling, it went back on the market at a substantially higher price – so we knew that, if we wanted to keep this unique piece of British history in the country, we had to raise nearly £360,000. That's way beyond our budget in the Museum, so we had to ask for funding from various different sources. The largest chunk came from the National Heritage Memorial Fund, which is the fund of last resort for the nation's heritage, coming to the rescue by funding emergency acquisitions. We managed to get most of the money together just a week before the deadline expired, and we rustled up a little bit more to make up the shortfall, and we got it, much to my relief.

> ... if we wanted to keep this unique piece of British history ... we had to raise £360,000 ... way beyond our budget

'As soon as we knew we'd managed to acquire the coin, we had a rush to get it on display as soon as possible. We put on a little exhibition here in the

Museum, and that opened the very next day! It stayed at the British Museum until July 2006 and then went to Norwich. After that it will tour to other venues, including Bedford Museum, close to where the coin was found; I like to think of the tour as Coenwulf's victorious royal progress around his kingdom.'

The rescue of the Coenwulf coin is a cautionary tale of what can happen to priceless objects that fall through the net of the Treasure Act. But there are structures in place now to help fill those gaps. The Portable Antiquities Scheme is the voluntary project run by the British Museum and the Museums, Libraries and Archives Council that encourages people to come forward and report archaeological objects that are not covered by the Treasure Act. Unlike the Treasure Act, its focus is not on enabling museums to acquire finds but on recording the information about these finds and their context, and making that available for public benefit. In this way it is building up a nationwide picture of finds, as for most objects it's the record of what they are and where they were found that is more important than what happens to the objects themselves.

The Portable Antiquities Scheme came into existence partly as a way of broadening public understanding of the importance of archaeological finds. At first piloted in six regions, it now covers the whole of England and Wales, and is gaining in recognition every month as more and more objects are brought forward, catalogued and, in some cases, acquired by museums. It's entirely voluntary, and there's no obligation on anyone to report their finds or to sell them to a museum.

'It's creating an important picture of what's found in the UK from the pre-historic period to the post-medieval era,' says Ian Leins, a curator of Iron Age and Roman coins at the BM, and formerly a finds adviser for the PAS. 'No one else is doing that. Local archaeological units will record what's found in their area, but the PAS builds up the national picture and fills in some of the gaps.'

The PAS works thanks to its network of finds liaison officers across England and Wales, some of them based in museums, some in local authority units, all of them administered by the British Museum and the Museums, Libraries and Archives Council. It aims to provide a one-stop shop for anyone who has found an object that they think might be of interest.

'Before PAS, the process was a bit hit and miss,' says Leins. 'You could take a find to a museum, but then you were relying on the expertise of the local curator, and there was no guarantee that what you'd found would come to wider notice. The PAS can take care of the find on every level. The first level of information relates to whether or not it's treasure; everyone needs advice

MUCH OF THE WORK I DO AT THE MUSEUM now is related to treasure. If you look in the cupboards in my office, you'll see that they're full of boxes of treasure. Hoards are coming in all the time, at a rate of about one a week, and we have to process them. You have no idea what to expect from one day to the next. Sometimes they're very run-of-the-mill hoards, just loads of examples of the same coin, but they still have a story to tell, and we have to deal with them as part of the process laid down under the Treasure Act.

A hoard can be anything from two gold or silver coins, which classify it as treasure, to massive hoards (500 isn't uncommon) of bronze coins. A man was digging in his garden in Gloucestershire in 2004 and he unearthed a large pottery vessel. As he dug around it, he realized it was massive, and it turned out to contain about 12,000 fourth-century Roman bronze coins. The definition of treasure in a case like this, where it's not precious metal, is ten coins or more – so you can imagine the alarm bells that went off with this find! A find of 12,000 coins is really panic time, because it can take so long to work through them all. In the event, they turned out to be nearly all the same type of coin; it was like counting modern money, such as a huge stack of 20p pieces. But you do get hoards where every coin is different, and that takes for ever to sort through.

Whatever the size of a hoard, curators have to go through the coins, identify them all to decide whether or not they're treasure, and write a report on them for the local coroner where they were found. Beyond that legal requirement, there's the academic interest: we have to record what's been found and where, and make that information available to scholars.

IAN LEINS
Curator of Iron Age
and Roman Coins

Every so often something turns up that has a huge impact. In 2003 a metal detectorist in Oxfordshire turned up a hoard that included a third-century Roman coin bearing the head and inscription of Emperor Domitianus II (about AD 271). It was a very important find because there are only fleeting references to Domitianus in written sources, and none says that he became emperor. This find proves that he was – or at least believed he was – even if it was only for a few days. After a flurry of interest, with the story even making headline news in *The Times*, the whole hoard was acquired by the Ashmolean Museum in Oxford, so it will be on display near to the area where it was discovered.

The Domitianus coin is a great reminder to us all that a very ordinary-looking hoard could contain something really important. The effect can be huge academically. So when I'm faced with a cupboard full of rather dull-looking hoards to process, I always bear that possibility in mind.

Above left and inset: Coins found by Ken Allen while digging a pond in his Gloucestershire garden.
Left: The third-century Roman coin found in Oxfordshire that confirmed the existence of a hitherto unknown emperor, Domitianus II.

BRONZE HEAD OF AUGUSTUS

I've always loved the bronze head of Augustus from Meroë, Sudan. We're used to seeing marble statues and portrait bronzes that look quite life-less, but this one really comes to life because of those glass and alabaster eyes, which just seem to pierce you as soon as you walk into the room. And it's not just any old head: this is a repre-sentation of a real man, a person whom we know a lot about. The identification of statues is also very interesting. Because they rarely have labels on them, we have to work out who they are by comparing them with other images and icono-graphy. You can compare this head to the heads that appear on Augustus's coins, and it's instantly recognizable.

IAN LEINS, *Curator of Iron Age and Roman Coins*

in that field. Say, for instance, you're digging out a pond in your garden, and you find three coins. You bring them to the PAS finds liaison officer and you'll find out what they're made of. If they're three gold coins, they're treasure, and you're obliged to declare them. If they're three bronze coins, they're not treasure.

'If your find turns out not to be treasure, then it's yours to keep. But the role of the PAS is to encourage people to report those things so that we can find out anything of value from them. The finds liaison officer will know if the object is of interest and can call on a whole range of specialist advisers, many of them from the British Museum. At that stage the object would be identified and photographed, and as much information as possible about the context of the find would be recorded. All that information goes on to the PAS database, which currently has about 250,000 objects on it – it's the largest catalogue of finds of its type in the world. It's accessible to everyone; that was always a very important part of the PAS mission, to make this information freely available to anyone who is interested. You might want to find out about things that have been discovered in your area, or look at objects of a certain type or period; the PAS database at www.finds.org.uk is fully searchable.

'Once the object has been recorded, it goes back to the owner. But we're finding that more and more people actually want their finds to go to museums. They get interested in the whole archaeo-logical process, and they realize that there's a value to these objects beyond their mere financial worth. So people are offering them for sale, or sometimes just giving them to museums outright.'

A good example of a wonderful object preserved for the nation through the Portable Antiquities Scheme is the Staffordshire Moorlands pan, a second-century AD copper-alloy vessel, 94 mm

in diameter, discovered by metal detectorists near Stoke-on-Trent in Staffordshire. As a single object made of non-precious metal, it's not treasure, but it's very beautiful, with its Celtic-style ornamentation inlaid with blue, red, turquoise and yellow enamel, and, like the Winchester hoard, it tells us a great deal about the time and place in which it was created. Below the rim runs an inscription MAIS COGGABATA VXELODVNVM CAMOGLANNA RIGORE VALI AELI DRACONIS, which instantly links the pan to the forts along Hadrian's Wall. The first four words are the Roman names for Bowness-on-Solway, Drumburgh, Stanwix and Castlesteads, all forts along the western sector of the wall, while RIGORE VALI AELI DRACONIS could mean that the bowl was made as a souvenir for a soldier called Aelius Draco or Dracon, who did military service on Hadrian's Wall.

'The Staffordshire Moorlands pan is a stunning object,' says Leins, 'probably a souvenir vessel of some sort, with a mixture of Roman and Celtic design elements to it, which tells us a lot about culture in the north of Britain in the second century AD. The people who found it were under no obligation to report it; they could have sold it in a car-boot sale, and we'd be none the wiser. But instead they took it to PAS, where it was identified and recorded, and as

Above: The Staffordshire Moorlands pan, a second-century souvenir of Hadrian's Wall, recorded through the Portable Antiquities Scheme and now jointly owned by a team of UK museums.

soon as word got out, there was a flood of interest. In the end it was jointly acquired by the British Museum, the Potteries Museum & Art Gallery in Stoke-on-Trent and the Tullie House Museum & Art Gallery in Carlisle. It's of both national and local importance, so it's nice that it will be displayed in all three museums. And that's a perfect example of the PAS really working.'

The PAS isn't just a passive recipient of objects; it also goes out and about encouraging people to bring their finds along for information and identification, like a rather highbrow version of *Antiques Roadshow*. PAS finds days have become extremely popular events, both around the country and in the British Museum, and they're an effective way of bringing the BM's expert curators into direct contact with the public.

'The finds days get people involved with the whole idea of archaeology and what a museum is for,' says Gareth Williams, who is regularly involved in finds days both in the British Museum and out on sites. 'We're not just saying to people, "Come along and let us record your finds." We're also saying,

... every new find helps us to piece together the bigger picture

"Help us to record the history of your area and your contribution to it." It's a way of letting people know how every little find contributes to the overall picture. If you have a very rich archaeological area, where there have been successive periods of occupation over a very long period of time, then every new find helps us to piece together the bigger picture. That's something that no museum can do on its own; we need everyone to get involved, and the Portable Antiquities Scheme makes that happen.'

5

Adding our bit to
the sum of knowledge

What the British Museum shows to its visitors – a collection of arte-facts from every culture and every period in history – is only half the story. While much of the Museum's time and money goes on the acquisition and preservation of the collection, there's another sphere of activity that the casual visitor could only guess at. Behind the scenes in Blooms-bury, and out on sites all over the world, the British Museum is engaged in a huge programme of research projects aimed at preserving human cultural history and deepening our understanding of it.

'People are surprised at how much research we do,' says BM director Neil MacGregor, 'and I think that's how it probably should be. When you come as a visitor, you want to engage with the things on display, helped by the information that goes with them. You don't want to think too much about the process whereby the objects and the information got there. It's like travelling by aeroplane: you just want to get on and ride; you don't want to think too much about how it works. But once you do start thinking about how it happens – about the generations of scholars who have discovered what these objects are, who made them, what they're for and what they mean – then you realize what a huge operation it really is. Every generation builds on the knowledge of the generations that have gone before. The most exciting thing about being the director of the Museum is trying to make sure that we add our bit to the sum of knowledge under this roof.'

All the curatorial staff at the British Museum are involved in research of one sort or another; the Museum is much like a university in that respect, and it enjoys the same kind of academic reputation. 'We're lucky in that we have access to the greatest collection of artefacts in the world,' says Dyfri Williams, Keeper of Greek and Roman Antiquities. 'Our job is not just to look after them and make sure that people can come and see them. We have to interpret them to the world as well. They're wonderful pieces of art that speak for themselves – but they're also capable of telling us about the history of the human race, the history of ideas and culture. In order to do that, we have to find out as much as we can about them and about the people who made them. Take the Greek vases, for instance. They're beautiful objects in their own right, both in their form and in the decoration. You could stare at them for hours.'

Above: Volunteer illustrator Mat Dalton draws a fragment of pottery from Naukratis, the Greek trading post in the Nile Delta.

Tiny objects, and those dug up by chance, provide material for British Museum researchers that can add significantly to the existing body of knowledge in a certain area. The Domitianus coin (see page 85) that was found in a hoard in Oxfordshire has rewritten Roman history by suggesting that there could have been an emperor whom nobody really knew about before. 'A simple thing like that can pop out of the Oxfordshire mud, and, once our researchers have done their job, it reveals a huge chunk of history,' says BM deputy director and head of research Andrew Burnett. 'It's not spectacular to look at – it's made of very poor metal – but it confirms the existence of a new Roman emperor.'

the Domitianus coin … has rewritten Roman history … there could have been an emperor whom nobody really knew about before

Research at the British Museum falls into six basic categories. Firstly, there's the cataloguing of the collections, a huge and continuing project that not only deals with new acquisitions, but also revisits things that have been in the collection for a long time, inputting new data into Merlin, the ever-growing online catalogue that will soon be made available to the public through the internet. Secondly, the Museum's collection must be looked at in terms of what is held in other collections, putting objects into a wider context that extends beyond London and the UK. There is also focused research that goes into mounting an exhibition or opening a new gallery, creating an exhibition catalogue and the interpretation material that will be seen and read by the public. There are also cross-cultural studies that look at objects from different areas of the collection in thematic terms: a new gallery about Time, for instance, takes a fresh, multi-disciplinary approach, just as the extant Living and Dying Gallery mixes artefacts from many different periods and cultures. Then there's fieldwork, comprising excavations both in the UK and overseas. Finally, there's research within the Conservation and Science departments, looking at new ways to extend the life of the collection and find out what things are made of and how they were created.

With such a huge diversity of research activity going on at any one time, it's important that the Museum has a clear picture of how best to focus its efforts and deploy its resources. While the Keepers, or heads of department, are responsible for the research that's carried out in their individual areas, they are now guided by the British Museum research board, which manages the overall research output of the Museum and makes sure each small project contributes to larger research goals. The board considers proposals, allocates money and shapes the Museum's larger goals at its monthly meetings.

'The research board came into being in 2005,' says Andrew Burnett, 'so we're really at the beginning of this initiative, but already we're seeing how we can shape all the individual efforts into bigger, more integrated projects. For instance, there's a lot of work going on in the Nile Delta, the Middle East and the Mediterranean – obviously those are incredibly rich archaeological areas. All those projects are shaping up into one much bigger piece of work about human settlement of the Mediterranean. It's not about stifling individual creativity, it's about making sure that our energies are focused so that we get the maximum public outcome from our work. That could be an exhibition, a publication, an education project or something on the website. A very important way of evaluating any project, whether it's a dig or an academic study, is what it could give us in terms of public access.'

The research board has identified three main headings under which the Museum's research work can be organized: the Mediterranean project, globalization, and religion and society. 'That's how we're shaping our agenda,' says Burnett. 'Obviously we won't force things, and every proposal will be judged on its own merits, but we need that overarching view, otherwise we'll all be pulling in different directions.'

Archaeological fieldwork accounts for much of the British Museum's research work, with major digs in Egypt, the Sudan, Turkey, Jordan and, when the political and military climate allows, Lebanon. There's also a considerable amount of fieldwork done in Britain, most of it following up treasure cases, such as the Ringlemere cup, a fabulous Bronze Age gold vessel unearthed in Kent in 2001. 'When something like the Ringlemere cup turns up we want to know everything we can about the site where it was found. Did it come from a grave? What else was associated with the find?' says J. D. Hill, secretary of the research board and manager of the Museum's archaeological activities. 'The cup itself dates from about 1500 BC, but excavation has shown that the cup was buried in the middle of a much older ceremonial monument. It also unexpectedly shows that 2000 years after the cup had been buried the site was chosen for an Anglo-Saxon cemetery because of its older associations. That's the joy and the headache of these sites: the minute you start digging, you find more and more questions.'

Another site that's proved to be exceptionally rich in research terms is Tutbury Castle in Staffordshire, home to fortified settlements since the Iron Age

That's the joy and the headache of these sites ... the minute you start digging, you find more and more questions

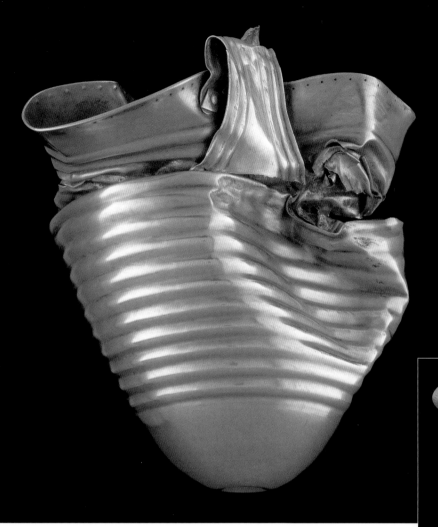

Left: The Ringlemere gold cup, a Bronze Age vessel (1700–1500 BC) found in Kent in 2001. Excavation of the Ringlemere site has revealed an early Bronze Age funerary complex; the cup may have been dislodged and damaged by modern ploughing. A computer reconstruction (below) shows its original shape.

or even earlier. Curator of Early Medieval Coinage Gareth Williams has been involved in the excavation of Tutbury for some years, and every time he goes back there he finds that the picture is getting more detailed. 'There's been a castle there since the Norman period, destroyed and rebuilt many times during the Middle Ages, and it's best known as one of the prisons that Mary Queen of Scots was kept in. It was partially destroyed during the English Civil War. So we've got a site that has been of strategic importance for thousands of years, with substantial archaeological remains and a great deal of documentary evidence in the form of letters and other written records. It's also linked with the Tutbury hoard, the largest hoard of coins ever discovered in England, which we know was removed from the castle in 1322 and found nearby in 1831. We're doing a long-term research project to put together the archaeological and written evidence to compile a definitive history of the castle and the surrounding area.'

Like all research projects, whether they're in a library, a laboratory or a muddy field, the Tutbury project is coming together slowly, like a jigsaw puzzle. 'We've been digging at the site for three years,' says Williams. 'The first year we found the corner of the foundations of a timber-frame building. That fits in with descriptions in Mary Queen of Scots' letters, where she says she's being kept in a "decrepit old hunting lodge" made of "wicked old carpentry". The remains we found were from the right date, and they were in the right part of the site, but we didn't know if this really was the building. In 2005 we worked along the wall and got to another corner, so we knew that it was pointing in the right direction, but we still don't know how long it was, and we had to be cautious about jumping to conclusions. In 2006 we followed the side wall for some distance, and it's the right size. That's conclusive. There can't be two buildings of that size in that place at that time, so we've got it. This is the prison of Mary Queen of Scots – and we know that it was a place where she was treated very badly.'

Further afield, British Museum staff have been excavating sites in the Middle East for many years. Jonathan Tubb is the curator of collections from the ancient Levant, and he's been working on a site in the central Jordan valley for over 20 years. Tell es-Sa'idiyeh, about 1.5 km east of the River Jordan, is a large, double mound (or 'tell') with settlement phases extending from the early Islamic period of the seventh century AD as far back at least as the Early Bronze Age of the third millennium BC.

'It was certainly occupied even earlier than that,' says Jonathan Tubb. 'We have evidence of settlement in the fifth millennium BC, so this is obviously a site that was very attractive to early farmers. The main settlement phase was Bronze Age, though, and that's when Tell es-Sa'idiyeh became a really important city. We've excavated a large palace complex that was destroyed by fire in approximately 2700 BC. It was a rambling complex of buildings, geared up for the production of commodities for export to Egypt. We've found evidence of olive oil, wine and textile production, and we know that during this period the economy of the Levant was based on export. So this palace housed a lot of artisans who were making it a very prosperous place indeed.'

The destruction of the palace complex on the lower of the two mounds may have been wrought by natural causes. 'There's evidence of earthquake damage,' says Tubb, 'and given the nature of the industrial activities on the site, particularly olive-oil production in buildings with timber roofs, the whole thing

> We've excavated a large palace complex that was destroyed by fire in approximately 2700 BC

could have gone up in smoke very easily. There's no evidence of people dying in
the conflagration, so it doesn't seem to have been an aggressive act. What we
did find in the public wing of the palace was a dining room and a small scullery
containing place-settings for 11 people, food platters and bowls which had
been ready to be washed up when the destruction took place. But there were
no human remains with them, so obviously the people had time to get out.'

The second major settlement phase at Tell es-Sa'idiyeh was in the twelfth
century BC, when the city, like much of the area, was under Egyptian control.
This time the main constructions were on the Upper Tell, where the British
Museum team has found the remains of a series of public buildings, including a
governor's residence, a palace with cisterns and storage rooms, and a state-of-
the-art water system. Meanwhile, the Lower Tell, site of that bustling Bronze
Age palace complex, was being used as a cemetery for those living on the
upper mound.

'The graves on the Lower Tell can reveal a lot about the way the people
on the Upper Tell were living,' says Jack Green, a special assistant on the Tell
es-Sa'idiyeh project, who is working on the publication of the cemetery

JACK GREEN

Special Assistant on the Tell es-Sa'idiyeh Project, with Jonathan Tubb (left), Curator of the Ancient Levant Collections

I'M WORKING ON THE PUBLICATION PROJECT for Tell es-Sa'idiyeh, pulling together a lot of the material about the cemetery site. I'm not employed directly by the British Museum; there are a lot of special assistants throughout the Museum who have the same kind of research input and who connect the Museum to other institutions around the world.

I was first given access to the Tell es-Sa'idiyeh material when I was doing my master's degree, and I realized its vast potential because there is no other burial site in that area that has such a wide diachronic range. When I started doing my PhD, I continued working on the Tell es-Sa'idiyeh material, and it's just carried on from there. I've got a grant from another funding body that allows me to carry on doing the work.

Having the opportunity to travel out to Tell es-Sa'idiyeh and actually examine the site is an amazing privilege. When you get there you see things about the physical nature of the site that you'd never get from a book. The landscape and topography really hit you. The bedrock on which the Lower Tell is built up is horseshoe-shaped. When filled with the silt from the earlier settlement, this provided an ideal terrain for a burial ground. And you can see that the site was easily defensible. Cities at that time would have been very vulnerable to attack from outside, so obviously if you're going to bury someone you want to do it in a place where you're not going to find people throwing spears at you. Also, you get a clear sense that the place of the dead was deliberately and symbolically separated from the place of the living – it's much lower down. That kind of thing adds a great deal to an academic understanding of a site.

I think the age of big, full-scale digs like this one is passing. It's partly to do with instability in the Middle East, where so many of the big sites are; it's also due to academic pressures to publish research papers. The major funding bodies want results much more quickly than they used to, and would prioritize the study and synthesis of the vast amounts of already excavated material. Perhaps that means we'll lose the traditional focus on large mound sites, sometimes known as 'tells' in the Middle East. So we'll have to look at a variety of interdisciplinary approaches that will broaden the scope of our work.

findings. 'In the graves, we tend to find whole objects that relate to fragments found in the Upper Tell. And they're usually in context with the human remains they were buried with. The cemetery was in use for a long time, so we can also see how burial practices and attitudes to death and the afterlife changed over the centuries. You can see the Egyptian influence very clearly. We have evidence of bodies being covered in bitumen and wrapped in linen, which is obviously some attempt at mummification.'

Grave goods, and the preparation of the body, can tell us a great deal about the sort of people interred on the Lower Tell. 'Objects were placed around the body as tokens of things they'd need in the afterlife,' says Green. 'It happens all over the ancient world, and it's much like taking flowers to a funeral today – it's a traditional practice that we don't really think about that much. Poorer people are buried with simple objects like a lamp and a bowl. People of higher rank have bronze vessels, lots of ceramic objects and all sorts of luxury goods. One very unusual burial has an individual placed face down, and over the back of his head have been placed three fish; we found their skeletal remains. A bronze bowl which was placed over his genitals, was swathed with textiles and contained a beautiful, ivory cosmetic box in the form of a Nile fish. It obviously meant something to somebody, but we don't know what. Fish symbolism is sometimes linked to death or fertility during the same period in Egypt, but in reality we know very little about religious practices in this area, so there's a lot of guesswork involved.'

> Objects were placed around the body as tokens of things they'd need in the afterlife

Some of the bodies have been found partially enclosed within ceramic *pithoi*, rather like clay coffins. '*Pithos*-burials are widespread across the ancient world,' says Green, 'and it shows that there were other funerary traditions coming into this area from neighbouring regions. Some of the bodies just appear to have their head in a ceramic jar or were simply covered in broken sherds. We think it might be the poor man's version of a *pithos*-burial, although this also suggests an intention symbolically to protect the body after death.'

Excavations have been under way at Tell es-Sa'idiyeh since 1985, and the project is now nearing its end. Results have been published throughout that time, and a full-scale publication is on the way. 'The final report really is the last word on this kind of long-term project,' says Jonathan Tubb. 'In the case of the cemetery, it will include every last detail, every grave photographed, drawn and described, all the finds discussed in terms of typology and parallels with other sites, all the human remains described. I've already published a lot about Tell es-Sa'idiyeh in academic journals, and I've included a summary of the main results of the excavations in my book, *Canaanites*. I lecture about the site all over the place, and try very hard to get the information out to the wider world as soon as I can.'

Above: An ivory cosmetic box in the shape of a fish from Tell es-Sa'idiyeh.

Sites like Tell es-Sa'idiyeh are an archaeologist's dream. 'What's most impressive about this project is that we have such a long period of continuous occupation, and we can bring chronological precision not only to the site itself but also to the entire region,' says Tubb. 'Even the graves assist in this process. Usually graves are just dotted around, with no chronological sequence. At Tell es-Sa'idiyeh we have new graves cutting into older graves, so we can put them into sequential order. Tell es-Sa'idiyeh was a major city, possibly corresponding to biblical Zarethan, which is mentioned in the Old Testament books of Joshua and Kings. There are very tangential mentions of the site in other sources, enough to tell us that this was an important place for a very long period of time.'

Y ou don't have to go all the way to the Middle East to explore the mysteries of the ancient world, however. The collections of the British Museum contain enough material to keep scholars busy for several decades to come. Some 130,000 inscribed clay fragments from ancient Iraq, covering a 3000-year period, came to the Museum in the nineteenth century and have yet to reveal all their secrets.

Some 130,000 inscribed clay fragments from ancient Iraq ... have yet to reveal all their secrets

'From an academic point of view, these fragments form one of our greatest treasures,' says Irving Finkel, curator of the Assyrian collections. 'They are fantastically informative, starting off with the beginning of writing in Mesopotamia and going right through to the second century AD. So far, about half of them have been cata-logued, and of those there are huge quantities that haven't yet been published. We have a fantastic amount of work to do.'

Nothing could exemplify more clearly than these Assyrian clay tablets the role the British Museum plays in solving puzzles from the ancient world. When they were first discovered in the early nineteenth century, the cuneiform writing that covers them, impressed in the wet clay by a stylus, then baked, was completely indecipherable. Now scholars can read it.

'In those early days of archaeology in the nineteenth century,' says Finkel, 'Iraq was under Turkish administration, and the deal was that anything that the British found out there came straight back to Britain. Nobody had seen anything like them before. Those languages – Akkadian, Sumerian and Babylonian – were as extinct as they could possibly be. But a group of determined people decided that they were going to read them, and they jolly well did. Much of the groundwork was done by an Irish cleric called Edward Hincks, who had a parish near Belfast and was the father of five daughters. He'd made great advances with Egyptian hieroglyphs, so when the Assyrian material arrived he thought he'd have a crack at that. What he achieved is absolutely amazing. Essentially, he deciphered Akkadian cuneiform, the ancient language of Babylon and Assyria. The intellectual achievement is staggering. In my opinion, it's much more impressive than the decipherment of hieroglyphs. They're easy: there's a box around the name, and once you've figured out the name, you're off. Cuneiform has no signposts like that. The fact that no one has heard of Edward Hincks is indicative of a problem in the perception of Mesopotamian material. Everyone with an interest in ancient cultures has heard of Jean-François Champollion, who cracked the Egyptian scripts. But to say that Hincks isn't a household name is an understatement. What Champollion did is trivial in comparison to Hincks's achievement.'

Once Edward Hincks and other scholars, such as Henry Rawlinson, had broken the code, the work of translating this massive body of literature could begin. 'There are two types of writing in the collection,' says Finkel. 'There's the stuff that was meant to survive – State and Church documents, royal and official records, literature and so on. Then there's a huge slew of private correspondence, written for the moment, concerning money, administration and law. From those two sides we get a great deal of information about how this civilization developed. There are history and mathematics texts, dictionaries, collections of medical cures and magic spells. Gradually all those pieces are squeezed through the mincer to get every bit of information we can, and we build up a picture of the Mesopotamian civilization that's every bit as interesting as any of the other ancient cultures.'

The star of the collection is without doubt the Gilgamesh epic, which was preserved on 11 clay tablets in the royal library of the seventh-century BC Assyrian king, Ashurbanipal, at Nineveh. Telling the story of the god–king Gilgamesh, supposed to have reigned in approximately 2500 BC, it's a racy tale of superheroes and monsters, sexy goddesses and male bonding that includes, among other things, an account of the great flood. 'The Epic of Gilgamesh is world-class literature,' says Finkel, 'and it comes to us entirely through this source. It's the sort of thing that you could sit in the

Above: Rev. Edward Hincks (1792–1866), the Belfast clergyman who in the 1850s successfully deciphered Akkadian cuneiform, the ancient language of Babylon and Assyria.

It's a racy tale of super-heroes … sexy goddesses and male bonding …

garden and read, and really enjoy. Its origins are in the storytelling tradition, but eventually it was written down in a standardized version, and that's what we have from the royal library.'

Such was the excitement generated by Gilgamesh that when George Smith, an assistant at the British Museum, first discovered the Assyrian version of the Old Testament flood story by reading the tablets, he 'jumped up and rushed about the room … and, to the astonishment of those present, began to undress himself'.

The translation of Gilgamesh and other treasures was not only contingent on the decipherment of the language – it also depended on the piecing together of many fragmentary sources. 'Puzzles are central to the study of inscriptions,' says Irving Finkel. 'Nearly all the tablets are broken. The royal library yielded about 20,000 pieces, and you have to find which bit goes with which. Most of the material was found in context after an act of violence, in this case the sacking of Nineveh in 612 BC by the Medes and Babylonians, who set fire to the library. The tablets were originally on shelves, all beautifully in order, but during the fire the floor caved in, and they crashed through to the room below. They were found, broken and baked in the fire, over 2500 years later. So a lot of the work is like putting together a very scattered jigsaw puzzle. We don't just sit around in white coats going, "Look! I found the bit that goes here!" and then all go out to lunch. The reassembly of the fragments is just the primary process. Then you take the inscriptions and find out what they mean – that's much more complicated.'

So what can the tablets give us, apart from some ripping yarns about gods and monsters? 'When archaeologists first started digging in Iraq, they had a very specific agenda, which was to find scientific proof of Bible stories,' says Finkel. 'That was very successful. In the nineteenth century, when everyone read their Bible, they were familiar with the names of kings, such as Solomon and Nebuchadnezzar, and that was the first point of interest. After that, we started to become interested in how the people of ancient Mesopotamia lived, how their civilizations developed and what they contributed to world knowledge. We have the discovery of writing and mathematics, some very basic things like the division of a minute into 60 seconds, the roots of modern religion and medicine. That's not bad going.'

The reassembly of this vast body of knowledge is a slow process. 'We have huge resources and very few workers,' says Finkel. 'There is endless work to be done and not enough scholars to do it. On a good day there are maybe 15 people in our study room, and I sometimes think that you could get all the

Opposite: The Flood tablet, one of the most famous fragments comprising the Epic of Gilgamesh.

IRVING FINKEL

Curator of the Assyrian Collections

A GREAT DEAL OF MY WORK IS ABOUT SOLVING PUZZLES, and of all the puzzles I've worked on the one that has taken over my life to the greatest extent is the Royal Game of Ur. It's a very remarkable thing, one of a set of game boards with dice and pieces that was discovered in the 1920s in southern Iraq, and dates from about 2600 BC. It's obviously some kind of race game, but we never knew how it was played. Then, early in the 1980s, I was swimming through the cupboards in the department, looking for interesting things, when I found a very odd-looking clay tablet marked with 12 boxes on one side, and cuneiform inscriptions on the other. I worked like mad to read it, and eventually I realized that it was rules for a game.

I translated the tablet and tried it out on various surviving games from the Middle East – one from Egypt, called senet, another one that looks like cribbage, and the Royal Game of Ur. I drew them all out and tried to find something that fitted – and the Royal Game was the one that worked. The rules made perfect sense. It doesn't actually say, 'Open the box and take out the pieces' – it assumed that you knew the basic game, and it gave a lot of rules about what you have to throw, how you bet and so on. It wasn't an innocuous parlour game: this was a serious bit of gambling. It's all couched in terms of getting enough beer, enough meat and enough women, and the pieces are called 'dogs', which means a gaming piece, but is also slang for a mercenary. So the rules are couched in terms of hungry, thirsty, randy soldiers competing to get what they want.

The board we have is from about 2600 BC, and we know that the game was played for a very long time before it was replaced by backgammon, which succeeded it in the Middle East and remains popular to this day. We discovered by chance that it survived right up to the present day in India. An anthropologist went to Cochin, the Jewish area of India, on a buying trip, and found a gaming board that was almost identical to the Royal Game of Ur. It came to light that there was a lady living on a kibbutz in Israel, where many Indian Jews from Cochin had settled, who knew how the rules worked and had played the game with her aunt in India. So here we have a game from the third millennium BC that survived to the end of Mesopotamian culture, then travelled with the Jews to India and survived to modern times.

Games have become a very large part of my life now. They're things that aren't taken very seriously, but have a tendency to survive for long periods of time and are diagnostic of the movement of people. They're usually about themes of racing or hunting, which are pretty universal. I'm now involved in a more or less global project to rescue traditional games before they vanish for ever. I tend to keep it quiet, though, because I don't like being introduced at British Museum parties as 'the man who plays board games'.

Above: Irving Finkel (centre) and colleagues at an exhibition celebrating the Royal Game of Ur in 2006.

people in the world who read Sumerian and Akkadian on one double-decker bus. If I had my way, any bright school-leaver with an interest in history and an aptitude for languages would be encouraged to study Mesopotamia. There's a massive focus on ancient Egypt: it's taught in schools, and you see programmes on TV all the time; we suffer in comparison. But what we have to offer is incredibly interesting: we have kings and emperors striding through palaces saying, "Off with his head!"; we have wealth and power and corruption and sex. From a Hollywood point of view, it's great. We want to raise awareness of the material in order to promote public understanding of the enormous contribution of the historic cultures of Iraq, especially given the current circumstances of that region.'

THE LEWIS CHESSMEN

My whole life has been tied up with the Lewis Chessmen: they're the reason I came to the British Museum, and they're my favourite things in the whole world. I grew up in one of those families where we were taken to the BM all the time, so I saw the chessmen when I was quite little – and I just thought they were wonderful. It's the faces: they look at you in this steady, slightly sardonic way. When you're a kid, you look at them eye to eye, and they go with you for the rest of your life. I've done a lot of work on them; I've written a book about them – it's just a pity they're not actually in my department!

IRVING FINKEL, *Curator of the Assyrian Collections*

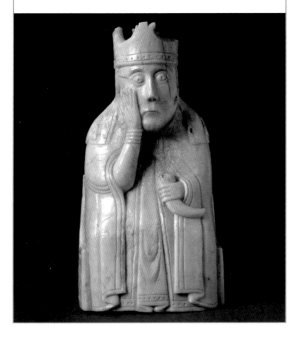

Among other headlines, a study of the Mesopotamian tablets shows the roots of monotheistic religions – and there are few things that shape the modern world more than that. 'Judaism, Christianity and Islam all have their roots in that part of the world, and they're all rooted in the religious practices that came before them,' says Finkel. 'The background is flourishing pantheism on a huge scale: big gods, little gods, local gods, a bewildering situation that the scribes tried to codify in sort of religious phone directories. But then we start to see that all the little gods are regarded as manifestations of the great god Marduk, and there are theological texts that point to the emergence of monotheism. At the time that Judaism was developing out of the theological life of Judaea, before and after the captivity, this was the religious background. The principal heritage of the ancient Near East is a crystallization of a polytheistic system into monotheism, and those monotheistic religions are as vibrant and influential today as they ever were.'

The British Museum's research programme is built essentially on a series of collaborations with other museums and institutions, sharing knowledge and skills across a wide and ever-developing body of scholarship. One endeavour that demonstrates this multi-disciplinary approach at its most vibrant is the Ancient Human Occupation of Britain (AHOB) project, a joint venture of the British Museum, the Natural History Museum and various universities, looking at evidence of our earliest ancestors in the British Isles. The project is searching for new evidence of the earliest human arrival in Britain, and analysing this and existing material to address questions of how people survived, what technology they developed and where they settled.

'We started off with the basic question of when did humans first get here,' says Nick Ashton, curator of the British Museum's Palaeolithic and Mesolithic collections, and the Museum's key figure in the AHOB project. 'From there, we move on to look at what happened to them. There appears to be a big gap in human habitation from 200,000 years ago to 60,000 years ago, when humans just seem to disappear from the record, so we need to test the validity of that observation. And we're looking at factors such as the creation of the English Channel – when we became separated from mainland Europe – as the reason for human absence. When humans did return, what were they? Were they Neanderthals? In what conditions did they live, and what material culture did they have?'

Above: The Happisburgh dig. It was thought that the oldest human sites in northern Europe were half a million years old. The findings at Happisburgh could double that figure.

The starting point for AHOB was a reunion of the collections of the British Museum and the Natural History Museum which were separated when the latter was created in the 1880s. 'Basically, the British Museum has the stone tools, and the Natural History Museum has the bones, teeth, antlers and environmental data,' says Ashton. 'We're building up a picture of ancient human occupation by looking at how those things go together, and returning to the sites where they were found to examine the evidence using the latest analytical methods.'

The findings have been rich, even though in terms of visual spectacle they don't offer much to the untrained eye. Much of the material analysed in the AHOB project is minute – pollen grains, for instance, or bits of fossilized wood. Those artefacts that do remain, such as stone handaxes or bits of bone and antler bearing cut-marks, are not among the Museum's most gorgeous possessions. But the implications of all these things when put together are far-reaching.

'We've been digging at Happisburgh on the Norfolk coast, where we've found two important new sites, which is very unusual. The pollen evidence, among other things, suggests that these human remains are much, much older than we ever thought possible. We used to think that the oldest human sites in northern Europe were half a million years old. The findings at Happisburgh could double that figure.'

The Happisburgh site has become the focus of intense activity. 'It was first discovered by a man walking his dog along the beach,' says Ashton. 'He saw what he thought was a handaxe coming out of the layer of organic mud on the foreshore. That's a very old layer, and as the north Norfolk cliffs crumble into the sea, fresh things are always being revealed. We started excavating the site, and we've found rich environmental evidence that helps date the handaxe. It's a great leap forward in our knowledge of ancient human life in this country.'

> It's a great leap forward in our knowledge of ancient human life in this country

The environmental evidence that can help archaeologists to date human artefacts offers a fascinating detective story in its own right. 'On the smallest level, there are pollen grains, which give a vegetational history of the site. Under a microscope we can identify the plant species, and we know when certain things became extinct, which enables us to date the pollen. Beetles give you a huge amount of climatic data because certain sorts of beetles will only live in certain temperatures, so if they're present, we have an accurate idea of the climate. Snails also give us evidence of the environment, and can be used for dating. All these methods go way back beyond the reach of carbon dating, which only works up to about 50,000 years ago.'

As well as organic materials, there is also the fossil record – and one of the most insignificant-looking fossil remains has turned out to be the most revealing. 'We learn a lot from fossilized voles' teeth. Because voles have such a short lifespan, they tend to evolve much quicker than other species. As they evolve, their teeth change shape, the thickness of the enamel changes, and they go from being an animal with rooted teeth to unrooted teeth. So depending on the type of voles' teeth that we find in a site, we can estimate the date. The teeth are really tiny, about the size of a clipping from your little fingernail, and we can only retrieve them by sieving through masses of sediment. We might have 10 tonnes of fairly intractable clay, which has to be dried out and then repeatedly sieved through very fine mesh. That might yield say a dozen voles' teeth. If we find teeth from a European pine vole, for instance, we know that the site is over 350,000 years old because that's when they disappeared from Britain. All these environmental elements taken together can give us a pretty accurate idea of the age of a site. At Happisburgh we have a combination of pollen, voles' teeth and geological evidence that's making us very excited. They're little things individually, but read together they mean a lot.'

6
Building the collection

There was a time when putting together a collection like that of the British Museum was both desirable and possible. In the eighteenth and early nineteenth centuries, antiquities were generally regarded as both movable and collectable, and the present idea that they were the property of a particular nation had not yet been born. True, when Parliament voted £35,000 in payment for the Elgin marbles there was a certain amount of disgruntlement, memorably recorded by the satirist George Cruikshank in a cartoon caption 'John Bull buying stones at the time his numerous family want bread'. But the money was spent, the 'stones' acquired for public display, and the Museum went on collecting. Ancient sites around the world were visited by inquisitive antiquaries and archaeologists, who brought some of the world's most famous objects to London for the Museum collection, stimulating worldwide public interest in the history of humanity.

In the twentieth century, even as countries around the world started to found national museums of their own, the British Museum continued to build up its collection with pieces legally exported or acquired on the open market. In the 1980s the annual acquisition budget was still £1.4 million, which was enough to sustain the collection and keep it dynamic and contemporary. At the same time, the Museum also supported international efforts by bodies such as UNESCO to curb the illicit trade in antiquities, and worked with museums worldwide on the protection of their heritage.

Now the acquisitions budget has shrunk to £100,000. Divided among the eight collecting departments, that's £12,500 each per year. It's enough to pick up a few nice bits and pieces, but when it comes to making serious acquisitions, Keepers and curators are obliged to look elsewhere for funding. Purchases have to be increasingly focused; the Museum can no longer buy things just because they're good. Any new acquisitions have to fill a perceived gap in the collection or tell a new story about the past for public benefit. The 'Queen of the Night' relief, the Old Babylonian clay plaque from around 1800 BC, tells an important story about ancient Middle Eastern religious beliefs. It represents a type of decorative work of which the collection had no good examples, so when it went up for sale in 2002 the British Museum decided to make it the principal acquisition for the 250th anniversary year. The plaque had been in England since the 1920s, and the current owner was trying to sell it abroad, but an export licence would not be granted. It was acquired for a sum of £1.5

Above: George Cruikshank's cartoon lampoons the acquisition of the Elgin marbles for a price of £35,000 in 1816. Lord Castlereagh (at left, in black hat) tries to persuade a distinctly unimpressed John Bull and his hungry family that the 'stones' are worth the money.

million, variously sourced from the Heritage Lottery Fund, the Art Fund and other donors. It's now one of the star exhibits in the Mesopotamian galleries.

The story of the 'Queen of the Night' is typical of how things come to the British Museum in the twenty-first century. Objects are either offered directly or go on the open market, bids are made, and, if they're successful, funds are gathered from a variety of sources. The objects, once acquired, are immediately put on prominent show in the Museum, giving instant access to the public for whom they were bought. The Coenwulf coin (see page 80) very nearly slipped through the net, but thanks to the persistence of BM curators and the generosity of various funding bodies, it was saved: purchased one day, on display in the Museum the very next day, before being taken on tour around the country.

'It's tempting to say that we've got enough already, that we should stick to our tiny acquisitions budget and not go to such great lengths to acquire new objects,' says BM deputy director Andrew Burnett. 'But we have a duty to future generations to keep on collecting. If something like the "Queen of the Night" becomes available, and it fills an important gap in our collection, we'd be neglecting our duty if we didn't try our hardest to obtain it. But things like that don't come along so often now. Ancient objects from foreign cultures can't be bought from abroad so easily;

> ... we have a duty to future generations to keep on collecting

they have to have been in the UK for a long time before we can acquire them. Most of what we acquire now is either British or contemporary. It's important that we keep buying contemporary work because if we don't get it now, we may never get the chance again. Future generations would wonder what we thought we were doing! We have to target our acquisitions very carefully, but then again, you can't just focus on high art. Things that seem like disposable rubbish today can be important in the future. We have a huge collection of eighteenth-century ticket stubs, for instance, which entered the Museum in 1799. People may have scratched their heads at the time, but now they're regarded as really important pieces of social history, telling us about how people spent their leisure time.'

Some acquisitions are delightfully simple: people just decide to give things outright to the Museum, and they don't cost a penny. Take the case of Charles Octavius Swinnerton Morgan (1803–88), vice-president of the Royal Archaeo-logical Institution and MP for Monmouth in South Wales. In his lifetime he amassed a major collection of clocks and watches, as well as scientific instruments, chamberlain's keys, papal rings and glass and ceramic items. He was a renowned horologist, a prolific writer and scholar. During his lifetime, he presented a number of valuable objects to the British Museum – and then, when he died, he bequeathed his entire collection of over 300 pieces. The Morgan bequest became the basis of the British Museum's world-famous collection of clocks and watches.

The Morgan bequest became the basis of the British Museum's world-famous collection of clocks and watches

'The generosity of donors like Octavius Morgan is breathtaking,' says David Thompson, head of the horological collection. 'In 1853 he came across a really extraordinary clock made in France in 1589. It's a beautiful thing, a miniature model of the cathedral clock at Strasbourg, about 5 ft high and fabulously decorated. When Morgan saw it exhibited at the Royal Society, he wrote to the British Museum saying, "I've been offered this clock for £100. I can buy it on your behalf if you are interested." And the trustees replied saying, "No, thank you!" So Morgan bought the clock for himself and took it home to Monmouthshire, where it lived in a case at the bottom of his stairs. And then, when he died, he left it to the Museum.'

The Habrecht clock isn't just a pretty face – although, with its lavish decoration of zodiacal signs, it certainly is beautiful to behold. It also tells an intriguing story about religious divisions in the sixteenth and seventeenth centuries. 'For many years it was thought to have been made for Pope Sixtus V,' says Thompson, 'because during the eighteenth and nineteenth centuries it was

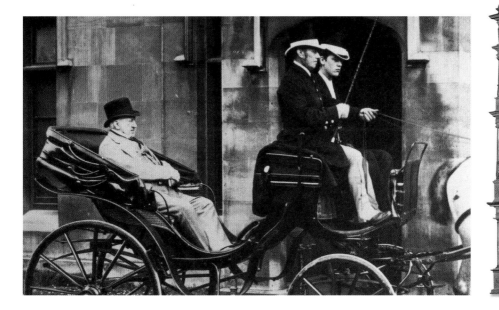

in the Vatican. The date of manufacture was documented, so people naturally assumed it was made for the pope of the day. But when we were doing some research on it a few years ago, we were working on the carillon, and we realized that two of the bells were wrong, so the clock played a chromatic scale rather than a Gregorian mode. Once the bells were corrected, it played a tune that was eventually identified as a setting of the Lord's Prayer by Martin Luther. So it seems that this clock, which lived in the Vatican for all those years, was actually a profoundly Protestant piece, playing music written by the father of the Reformation.'

While old objects continue to come into the British Museum's collection, it's in the area of modern and contemporary collecting that the acquisition programme is, perhaps, at its most vital and interesting. Judy Rudoe is responsible for the Modern collection of nineteenth- and twentieth-century applied arts from Europe and America, including jewellery, silver, metal-work, ceramics and glass. 'Ever since its foundation in 1753, the British Museum has acquired contemporary artefacts,' she says. 'One of Josiah Wedgwood's famous copies of the Portland Vase was given to the Museum by his son, and it's important that we keep acquiring the best representative pieces of modern design to carry on that tradition. That's what the Modern collection, as it's known, is all about.'

> ... it's important that we keep acquiring the best representative pieces of modern design

DAVID THOMPSON

Head of the
Horological Collection

I'M THE HEAD OF THE HOROLOGICAL COLLECTION – clocks and watches and anything that ticks, basically. We have something like 900 clocks and 4500 watches in the collection, of which only about 300 pieces are on display. But anyone with a serious interest can come into the study room and look at the collection. It really is the best in the world. We don't acquire so much now, just the occasional modern piece. If something good comes up at auction, we might try to bid for it, but we don't have the resources to compete. Fortunately, due to the generosity of our great benefactors, such as Octavius Morgan, we have pieces that cover most of the important periods of clock-making. The only thing we're desperately awaiting is Harrison's missing timekeeper!

I started out as a complete amateur. I was working in a classical music shop in the 1970s, but I'd always been interested in horology, so I left my job and went to study clock- and watch-making at Hackney College. When I graduated I got a job at a restorer's in Clerkenwell in central London. I'd only been there for a few weeks when the British Museum advertised a six-month temporary job working on the Horological collection. I applied, and one afternoon the phone rang and I was offered the position. My boss was very understanding; he said he'd hold my job open for me for six months, and if I didn't like the British Museum I could come back to him. That's 27 years ago now; I never did go back. So I owe my position here to my wife, who supported me for two years while I was a student at Hackney, and my first boss, who let me give up a good job to go and play at the British Museum for six months.

The impetus to expanding the decorative arts collection from the nineteenth century onwards came from an extraordinary gift made to the British Museum in 1978. Anne Hull Grundy, heiress to the Mettoy fortune (which derived from manufacturing toys, such as Corgi cars), had been collecting eighteenth- and nineteenth-century jewellery since the 1940s, and in 1978 she contacted the Museum with the news that she intended to donate the lot.

'It amounted to around 1200 pieces of jewellery,' says Rudoe. 'Mrs Hull Grundy had read the catalogue of an exhibition that the Museum did in 1976 – *Jewellery through 7000 Years* – and she realized that our collection petered out in about 1700. So she deliberately set about acquiring objects from the eighteenth century onwards in order to drag our collection up to date. In 1978 she announced that she was going to give it to us, and it took us slightly by surprise. She started sending it up to us by taxi from her home in Hampshire, wrapped up in old Kleenex boxes, or her husband's cigar boxes. There was no order to the way in which she sent it. We never knew what was going to come in from one day to the next: a wonderful Art Nouveau piece by René Lalique or a superb piece of eighteenth-century diamond jewellery. We got the whole collection listed and on display by the end of the year, and then we set about writing the catalogue.'

Anne Hull Grundy was among the more remarkable of all the Museum's benefactors. Born Anne Ullmann in Nuremberg, Germany, in 1926, she was raised in a wealthy, cultivated Jewish banking family. In 1933, with the rise of the Nazis, the family moved to England, and little Anne started buying bits and pieces of jewellery with her pocket money (her acquisitions would be picked up by the family chauffeur). In 1947, at the age of 21, she married John Hull Grundy, an artist and entomologist 20 years her senior, who encouraged her collecting mania and led her to take a more scholarly interest in the things that caught her eye.

'Their marriage is a very strange story,' says Judy Rudoe. 'They met when Anne was 17, and she married him as soon as she possibly could, apparently to get away from her parents. Then she appears to have fallen ill soon afterwards. She went around in a wheelchair for a while, before becoming permanently bedridden in her late 30s. She remained in bed for the last 20 years of her life, but that didn't stop her collecting. She'd do all the buying and selling from her bed, she'd get her favourite dealers to come down from London, and she'd do a huge amount of business by phone and letter. She was as eccentric as they come, but she certainly knew what she was doing. She bought fabulous eighteenth-century gem-set pieces, nineteenth-century pieces by the great English, French and Italian designers – Burges, Fontenay, Castellani – as well as Tiffany of New York and wonderful Art Nouveau. A lot of the things she

This table clock was made around 1690 by the English clock-maker Thomas Tompion for the royal bedchamber of William III. It's an astounding piece of horology because it actually runs for a whole year on one winding. To make a clock go longer you have to add a wheel, and every time you add a wheel, you have to increase the power of the mainspring, and if you're not careful, there's so much force that the whole thing will either explode or jam up. This clock has been running smoothly, as far as we know, since 1690. After the king's death it was given to a gentleman of the bedchamber, Henry Sydney, Earl of Romney, and passed by descent through the lords of Mostyn until it was purchased for the Museum in 1982.

From 1798, the lords Mostyn kept a record book, noting the annual winding of the clock, and they threw a party to celebrate the event, at which everyone, including the lord, his guests and the servants, had a go at turning the key. We've resumed that practice, and we have an annual clock-winding party in early February each year. Winding the clock can take up to an hour, depending on how many people are at the party!

DAVID THOMPSON, *Head of the Horological Collection*

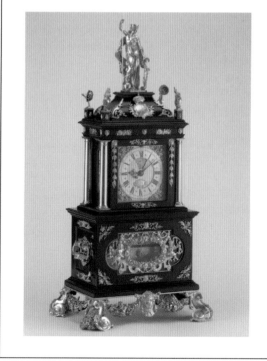

JUDY RUDOE

Curator of the Modern
Collection of
Nineteenth- and
Twentieth-century
Applied Arts from
Europe and America

I STARTED AT THE BRITISH MUSEUM in 1974 as an assistant curator. The arrival of the Hull Grundy gift in 1978 really turned my life around, and I learnt as much as I possibly could from it. Then, in 1986, I took over responsibility for the Modern collection. These great opportunities don't come along often, and you have to grab them when they do.

I try to broaden the range and depth of the Modern collection as much as possible within the limitations of our purchasing power. One of the areas I really wanted to build up was twentieth-century American design, so whenever I was in New York I started combing shops in Soho and Greenwich Village looking for pieces by designers like Russel Wright and Eva Zeisel. There were things I could pick up for a few dollars, wrap them up in tissue paper and bring them back in the overhead locker – economy class, of course! If colleagues were going over to New York, I'd say, 'Oh, I need the gravy boat from this Russel Wright service, or the Eva Zeisel salt cellars – I'll pay you when you get back!'

When they started the Modernism fairs at the Armory in New York, I made some wonderful acquisitions. You have to buy these things on the hoof and hope that the Museum will approve when you get them home. I'm willing to spend up to about £1000 of my own money; it's a risk because the keeper could say I'd gone completely mad, but it hasn't happened yet.

I've been collecting a lot of work by Eva Zeisel: she's a living legend of the twentieth century, a Hungarian designer who worked in Germany in the 1920s and Russia in the 1930s, before moving to New York just before the Second World War. She was 100 years old in 2006. When I first met her she was so taken with the fact that I was buying her ceramics for the British Museum that she started giving me things, and now every time I visit her she presses something into my hand. She's a wonderful designer, starting out at the time of the Bauhaus, but rejecting what she saw as their clinical approach; all her work is bold, bright and compulsively tactile.

Sometimes a piece will turn up at a selling exhibition, and I have to move very quickly in order to get it. In 2000 a London dealer announced that he had an early 1930s' Eva Zeisel coffee set; this was something that we'd wanted in the collection for a long time. I got back from a trip to New York on a Saturday night and found this dealer's catalogue on my doormat. The exhibition opened on the Tuesday, and I knew he worked on a first-come, first-served basis. I rang him and begged to be allowed to come in advance and see the coffee set – just to make sure it was the set I really wanted. He agreed – and it was. So there was nothing for it, I had to get there two hours early on the day of the sale and wait for the doors to open. I was the second in the queue, and I was worried that the woman in front was after the same thing. We got chatting and as soon as I discovered we weren't after the same thing I could relax. The doors opened, I steamed in and said, 'Mine!' and bought it for £650.

bought were extremely unfashionable – all that Victorian jewellery had gone right out of favour in the 1960s and 1970s – so she was able to put together an impressive collection at a reasonable price. We couldn't begin to think of acquiring that material now. And she gave us the whole lot! The only condition was that we'd show it and produce a scholarly catalogue. Which we did! She was breathing down our necks the whole time, calling up, sending postcards saying, "Where's my catalogue?" We worked as quickly as we could, and the two-volume catalogue came out just after her death in 1984. It was sad that she missed it. I think it would have given her a great deal of pleasure.'

Unfortunately, not every new acquisition in the Modern collection is handed to the Museum on a plate. Most things have to be bought, and, with the acquisitions budget so much lower than it used to be, Rudoe and other colleagues throughout the Museum have to use other sources, specially targeted for the purpose. 'Our purchasing power in the 1980s was fantastic,' she says. 'At its height, the special budget for modern applied art was £25,000 a year. Then it went down to £14,000, then £10,000, then nothing – and that's when I went to the British Museum Friends!' The BMF – a membership organization for people who support the work of the Museum and pay an annual subscription – funds acquisitions and research programmes throughout the British Museum, and it came up with a 'running fund' of £5000 a year, earmarked specifically for the Modern collection. The point of a running fund is that it enables spontaneous acquisitions to be snapped up at antiques fairs without needing approval by a lengthy committee.

'As a result of the Hull Grundy gift bringing our jewellery collection into the twentieth century, we decided that we'd extend the dateline in other areas

BASSE-YUTZ FLAGONS

These Iron Age flagons from France have the most distinctive shape and design, and I can't go through the gallery without stopping and looking at them. They were made in about 400 BC, but they look to me as if they could have been produced in the twentieth century. It's wonderful to see that sort of continuity, how designers throughout the ages have come to the same conclusions about form and function and created something very beautiful. They first came here in the 1920s, and they caused so much interest that a firm in Staffordshire started making pottery copies of them. Objects in the Museum have always inspired modern craftsmen, and I love the idea that we're a source of design ideas.

JUDY RUDOE, *Curator of the Modern Collection of Nineteenth- and Twentieth-century Applied Arts from Europe and America*

in which we were already strong,' says Rudoe. 'We've built on our earlier ceramics, glass and metalwork. My predecessor, Michael Collins, left in 1986, and since then it's been my responsibility to keep the Modern collection going. In recent years the only way I've been able to do that is with help from the BMF running fund, which was a lifeline until the budget went back to the central acquisitions fund. Now we're in a position where we have a set budget, which is still only £5000, but we can go to the Friends if we need to top it up for a specific purchase. We also go to the Art Fund and other funding bodies. Putting these funds together can be a massive job. I work six days a week as it is, and that's mostly on all the other aspects of my job.'

Sometimes, of course, the BM can't do it all by itself. In 2005 an important collection of gold and silver objects formed by German-born British merchant banker Sir Ernest Cassel (1852–1921) was offered for sale, but no single British museum was in a position to acquire the whole lot. So the British Museum joined a consortium, led by the Ashmolean Museum in Oxford and the Victoria & Albert Museum in London, that arranged to buy pieces according to the special relevance they would have to the various institutions. With support from the National Heritage Memorial Fund, the Art Fund and other bodies, the British Museum acquired the Palmerston gold chocolate cups, a pair of delicate, early eighteenth-century drinking vessels that once belonged to the first Viscount Palmerston. They're remarkable things, made from gold melted down from mourning rings inherited by Anne Houblon, Lady Palmerston.

'Mourning rings were given and worn in remembrance of deceased loved ones in the seventeenth and eighteenth centuries,' says Rudoe. 'These cups were made from rings inherited from her father or brother. Translations of the Latin inscriptions inside the handles read: "Let us drink to the dead" and "He has not deserved sweet unless he has tasted bitter". As chocolate was a fairly

Above: The Palmerston gold chocolate cups were acquired in 2005 with the support of the Heritage Lottery Fund, the Art Fund and private donations.

bitter, medicinal drink in those days, you can imagine Lady Palmerston and her husband sipping away in touching deference to their dead relatives. They're beautiful things but rather morbid, and they tell us a lot about attitudes towards death and grieving at that time.'

Gifts are still made to the Museum: for many artists and manufacturers, having a piece in the BM confers a status that no amount of advertising could achieve. But every so often something just comes out of the blue.

'I got an e-mail from the British Council one day, saying that a company in Moscow had commissioned a set of plates in the style of Russian revolutionary porcelain of the 1920s, and they wondered if we would like them. I e-mailed back asking for more information, and it turned out that the company in question was one of the very big energy conglomerates in Russia, Integrated Energy Systems. Their vice-president had been on a visit to London and had seen our collection of original plates, which were made after the 1917 Revolution to disseminate the slogans of the new republic. He'd realized, seeing those plates given such status in the British Museum, that this was a tradition

Above: One of a set of 12
plates commissioned by
Integrated Energy Systems
in Moscow in 2006.
Right: One of the British
Museum's 1920s' Russian
revolutionary plates that
inspired the creation of
the new set and the decision
to donate it to the Museum.

worth reviving, so he'd gone home and commissioned a new set commemorating the history of electrical energy in Russia from the 1880s to the present day. Once I found out the history and saw the pictures, I very quickly said, "Yes, please, we'd like them!" It's a great example of an old tradition being revived to serve the needs of the present day: in modern Russia, which is rebuilding itself after the fall of communism, the idea of a reliable electricity supply is just as important as it was when Lenin conceived his plan to electrify the USSR in 1920. And this new set of plates was inspired directly by objects in the British Museum's collection, so it says something about the Museum as a repository of world cultural traditions. We're an international custodian of culture. We give other countries a perspective on how their artefacts are perceived. And I think this is a very good way of answering questions about national ownership of artefacts.'

A principal area of contemporary collecting is in the department of Prints and Drawings, where Rembrandt, Dürer and Michelangelo share shelf space with Tracey Emin, David Hockney and Jake and Dinos Chapman. 'The Modern collection of prints and drawings starts in the 1880s with the work of Van Gogh and Seurat, and covers the whole of the twentieth century up to the present,' says curator Stephen Coppel, who is in charge of this area. 'The collection at the British Museum is best known for the Old Masters, but it's very important that we continue to acquire modern works on paper in order to perpetuate the collection as a great place of reference for future generations. Many artists would like their work to be represented here; it's up to us to ensure that the work we acquire is of sufficient importance and quality on historical and aesthetic grounds to justify inclusion. The collection is built for posterity. Every generation of curators leaves its trace on the collection through acquisitions made over a period of time, and we all have different tastes and interests – that's what gives the collection its richness and diversity. But we're all thinking of our duty to the future.'

> … it's up to us to ensure that the work we acquire is of sufficient importance and quality … to justify inclusion

The core of the Modern collection is a bequest by Campbell Dodgson (1867–1948), from 1912 to 1932 the Keeper of the department, who privately collected modern work precisely because he was aware that the British Museum was not acquiring it. 'Campbell Dodgson put together a very important private collection of prints by Redon, Pissarro, Manet, Gauguin, Munch, Toulouse-Lautrec and others,' says Coppel. 'They were collected with the specific aim of leaving them to the Museum, which is what he did when he died in 1948. That bequest of more than 5000 items formed the cornerstone of our modern holdings. Then nothing much happened in the 1950s and 1960s, until Frances Carey was appointed assistant Keeper of the Modern collection in 1975. With Antony Griffiths, the present Keeper of the department of Prints and Drawings, she initiated a series of groundbreaking exhibitions and publications designed to draw attention to the Modern collection, starting in 1978 with an exhibition of French lithographs from the Campbell Dodgson bequest. From that point on, the department directed its modern acquisitions towards developing particular areas of the collection, culminating in an exhibition and publication. This policy provided the impetus for the Modern collection to grow. We've focused on American prints, on German expressionist works, on the British avant-garde, on Picasso and the School of Paris, on modern Scandinavian prints and so on.

IN RECENT YEARS I've been building up a collection of Australian works – my ambition is for the British Museum to have the best collection of Australian works on paper outside Australia. When I joined the British Museum in 1992 we had very little, and nothing at all by one of the most significant twentieth-century artists, Fred Williams, who died in 1982. When I visited Australia in 1996 I met his widow, Lyn Williams, and purchased two prints. She gave me two more as a gift for the Museum, and we included them in an exhibition of new acquisitions. Lyn was so pleased with how Fred's work looked here that she decided she wanted to have his work represented in depth. In 2002 she gave us 70 etchings, which I selected, and nine related drawings, watercolours and gouaches, from the 1950s right through to the 1970s. The gift was made without any request for an exhibition. It was extraordinarily generous. A year later, in 2003, we produced an exhibition and catalogue of the Williams gift, which has acted as a catalyst for developing the Australian collection. Support has come from many other generous donors, and this will lead to an exhibition and catalogue at the end of the decade. The Gordon Darling Foundation in Melbourne and James Mollison, the founding director of the National Gallery of Australia, have been particularly helpful.

Another of the great donations to the department was the collection of David Brown. He had been a distinguished veterinary scientist in Africa, then he switched careers after the tragic death in Nigeria of his companion Liza Wilcox, and became an art historian, coming here to the BM to study works on paper. After graduating in art history from the University of East Anglia, he immediately got a curatorial post at the Scottish National Gallery of Modern Art, and shortly after at the Tate in London, where he worked from 1974 until his retirement in 1985. He was a great collector in his own right, and when he died in 2002 he left his collection of some 230 works on paper to us, including major gouaches by Roger Hilton, postcard sculptures by Gilbert and George, and early conceptual works by Richard Long and Hamish Fulton. He also left us half the proceeds from the sale of his London house for the purpose of extending the collections. That money, which is administered by the Art Fund, is now earmarked for the acquisition of works on paper by modern British artists. It's a wonderful way of remembering an incredibly generous man.

STEPHEN COPPEL

Curator of the Modern Collection of Prints and Drawings

'Exhibitions are important because they allow the public to see what we're acquiring, and they are a great incentive for people to donate to the Museum, either in terms of objects or money for acquisitions. Nearly all our acquisitions now are funded by external sources: our collection of modern Italian prints, for instance, which will be shown in 2007, has been built up over the past five years with funds provided by an anonymous donor. In 2001 the Rootstein Hopkins Foundation gave £500,000 to the BM to set up a trust fund for the purchase of works on paper by living British artists or those who have died within the past ten years. This is our principal source of funding for contemporary British works on paper, and has enabled us to acquire works by artists from the 1960s and 1970s, such as Patrick Caulfield and Antony Donaldson, both of whom had not hitherto been represented, as well as recent drawings by Richard Deacon, Tim Head and Hew Locke. We have to present our wares, so to speak, if we want people to help us to build the collection for the future.'

It's been a notably successful policy, attracting a series of gifts and bequests that makes the British Museum's collection of works on paper the envy of the world. And there was no more spectacular bequest than that of Alexander Walker (1930–2003), the respected author and film critic, who left the Museum his entire collection of more than 200 modern prints and drawings. The list of artists reads like a history of modern art: Picasso, Matisse, Miró , Dubuffet, Vaughan, Nevinson, Guston, Johns, Hockney, Hodgkin … The list goes on and on.

The list of artists reads like a history of modern art

It was certainly a very nice present – but why would an individual who has spent his life amassing such a valuable collection decide to give it all away after his death? 'Alex was a friend of mine,' says Stephen Coppel. 'I met him in the mid-90s – he was a great art lover, as well as being a prolific writer, and I'd often run into him at gallery openings. I would invite him to come to the Museum to the opening of our exhibitions, and moreover to come to our Friends' evenings in the department of Prints and Drawings. They're very informal affairs, where we lay out all the new acquisitions in the study room after hours, and they attract a lot of interest. Alex enjoyed these evenings immensely, and they gave him ideas for his own collecting.

'Eventually, he invited me to visit him at his London flat in Maida Vale to see what he'd got. I had no idea what to expect; I knew he collected, but nothing could prepare me for what I saw. It wasn't a big flat – and every single vertical surface was hung with something. There was a Chuck Close hanging

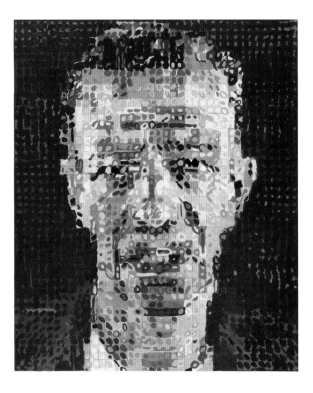

Three prints from the collection of the film critic Alexander Walker, who left more than 200 modern prints and drawings to the British Museum in 2003.
Above: Chuck Close's 1991 woodcut *Alex*.
Above right: Keith Vaughan's 1964 gouache *Cymbeline II: Fear No more the Heat of the Sun*.
Right: Lucian Freud's 1994 etching, *Reclining Figure*.
Opposite: Walker surrounded by his prints at his London flat in 2002, photographed by Rob Carter.

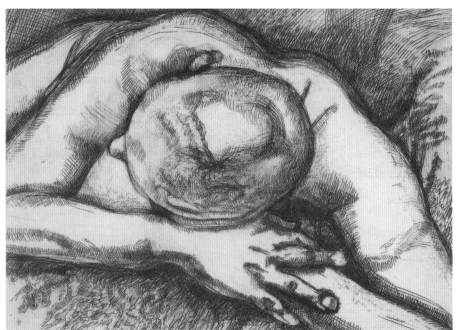

near the cooker, a Rachel Whiteread gouache above the bath, and between the kitchen sink and the windowsill there was a wonderful little Matisse etching. On the back of the bathroom door was an ink-and-brush drawing by Avigdor Arikha, a self-portrait of the artist screaming in a rage. In the cupboard that housed the vacuum cleaner there was a Jasper Johns lithograph. Alex actually apologized to me for the state of the flat! At the end of that first visit, he asked me if the British Museum would be interested in these works. I was totally taken aback. His collection fitted like a glove with the areas in which we were collecting.

'From that point on, I think Alex started to buy things with an eye towards how he could best help build the Museum's collection. In the last five years of his life, his buying became a lot bolder. He'd call me for advice when he was considering a purchase, and he'd invite me over to "welcome" a new piece. It was clear that he wasn't just buying for his own pleasure any more; he was buying for posterity.'

Below: Avigdor Arikha, *Self-portrait, Shouting One Morning*, a brush and sumi ink drawing from 1969.

Walker died suddenly in 2003; within a year of his death the British Museum had catalogued the entire collection and was ready to mount an exhibition of some150 works from the bequest. One of the people who came to the opening in 2004 was the Paris-based Israeli artist Avigdor Arikha, who saw his own work among the exhibits. Coppel recalls: 'Arikha was so pleased to be part of the show that he went up to Neil MacGregor and said, "This is the place where I want the work I've kept back for 40 years to come!" So Arikha, in his turn, donated 100 works on paper from 1965 to 2005, and in 2006 we mounted an exhibition of those works in the Museum. It's a perfect example of how gifts and exhibitions can inspire people to support our work and add to our collections.' A selection from the bequest is touring nationwide because of the enthusiasm generated by the show at the British Museum.

7
A place for learning and debating

Museums have a staid reputation for some people: they're seen as repositories for extinct cultures and dead ideas. A visit to the British Museum shows that it's anything but a cultural mausoleum; it's never been so proactively engaged with the thorny issues of the day. During the summer of 2006, for instance, there were simultaneous exhibitions exploring artistic traditions in the Middle East and homosexuality in ancient Rome. Any visitor expecting a passive, non-confrontational encounter with a few nice antiques was in for a shock: here were two of the big debates of the day writ large in the Museum's galleries. But is this really part of the Museum's job? Director Neil MacGregor thinks so.

'The British Museum was created in the eighteenth century as a civic space, a place for learning and debating. That's something we must reinvent in today's terms. One of the great achievements of the Museum lies in extending the academic understanding of different societies into the arena of public debate – that is the major outcome of all our work here. Exhibitions and galleries aren't just collections of beautiful objects. They're designed to get people thinking about all sorts of issues and, ultimately, thinking about their own lives.'

The job of the Museum, then, is to identify these cultural 'faultlines' and explore the way in which other societies have dealt with the same issues. 'The biggest lesson that we can learn from the study of ancient cultures is that human societies have always had to confront the same issues,' says MacGregor. 'We all deal with issues about death, growing old, sex, religion, love, political power and so on. The questions remain the same, but the range of responses can vary quite a lot. The only real question is where you fall in the spectrum in any given generation. It's very easy to believe you're confronting these issues for the very first time and to forget that it's all been done before. There is something both strengthening and stilling about knowing that other societies have thought these things through before you. Whatever we are struggling with as a society now, other societies have struggled with 1000, 2000, 5000 years ago. And they found some sort of solution.'

Despite its upfront engagement with contentious issues in the twenty-first century, the British Museum has not always been so keen to confront the implications of its collection. For many years, material that was deemed to be

Above: Figure of Dionysos from the east pediment of the Parthenon in Athens. Opposite: Visitors in front of the façade of the Nereid monument from Xanthos.

Opposite top: Thomas Bruce, 7th Earl of Elgin (1766–1841), who commissioned the removal of the Parthenon friezes. He spent a fortune shipping the sculptures to England, only to discover that Parliament would not pay the sum he was asking for them. Opposite below: Horsemen from the west frieze of the Parthenon, 438–432 BC.

obscene was kept from public show and only started to filter back into the general collections after the Second World War. So what's changed?

'If you look back 50 years,' says MacGregor, 'we had a very stable society in which very little of fundamental importance was being questioned in the mainstream. The big, seismic changes that came in the 1960s were bubbling up from the underground, but they weren't yet in the wider arena. So the discussions that we now have about religious or sexual identity could not have happened in the 1950s. The Museum is there for the public to use and has to reflect the attitudes of the changing generations. The public now wants to use the Museum in a different way, and our job is to decide how best to present the collection so that it can. At the moment, we're in a time of intense debate about all aspects of our culture, and it's our job to put the objects on show, open up debate and leave the conclusions open. In fact, I think one of our main objectives is to complicate issues. Every issue is usually much more complicated than it first appears, and if you start to look at the way that other cultures have dealt with it, you start to realize that.'

Everything in the British Museum's collection raises fundamental questions about human experience, whether it's a fabulously ornate clock or a rough-

> Everything in the British Museum's collection raises fundamental questions about human experience

hewn handaxe. But some objects have become the focus of particular debate, not simply because of what they tell us about the human condition, but also because people question whether or not they should be in the Museum at all. 'The two big issues that we are constantly having to arbitrate are the national "ownership" of a small number of objects and the status of human remains in the collection,' says MacGregor. 'We constantly review all the contentious issues, especially as the law changes and demands a response from us. Because of the nature of the collection – human artefacts from all over the world and from every period of time – those questions are never going to go away. We have a duty to think about what our responses are to those questions and to act on them in a way that balances the long-term value of the collection with the just claims of individuals.'

Debate about the national ownership of objects stems from a period of collecting when export laws were very different, and archaeologists and collectors were able to acquire antiquities abroad and bring them home. Things have changed now, and in most cases ancient finds stay in their country of origin, but that doesn't alter the fact that the British Museum, and other collections throughout the world, have a large number of pieces that once came from abroad. Some people feel that museums do not have the right to retain those pieces.

'The Museum must always arbitrate among the demands of different groups,' says MacGregor. 'In terms of cultural identity and the use of culture, there are effectively two, opposed positions. On the one hand, you can see culture as belonging to the whole of humanity, demonstrating how alike and interconnected we all are and therefore properly residing in an encyclopedic museum that is open to the whole world. On the other hand, you can see culture as something that defines a particular group of people, who have particular rights over it and should therefore be able to use it as they prefer. There is no easy compromise between those two positions. The most publicized issue about repatriation concerns the Elgin marbles, and it's a perfect embodiment of the debate

between the national and universalist views of culture. Basically, it's a tension between an eighteenth-century Enlightenment view of culture and a nineteenth-century view stemming from European Romantic nationalism. And that's a very important debate that can never be fully resolved. Obviously, the British Museum has its roots in the eighteenth-century universalist world view, but we can't just ignore the other position. What we can do, however, and this is a very exciting possibility, is to make those objects accessible to a much wider public. Technology in the last 30 years has made it possible for those objects to travel much more safely, so we can meet different needs in different places without compromising the long-term integrity of the collection. It's no longer a question of either keeping something or giving it back. Now we have different ways of sharing things, which actually enrich the meaning of the individual objects, letting them tell many different stories by allowing them to be seen in many contexts.'

This concept of shared access seems, for many, to be the way ahead. Author Vikram Seth, a trustee of the British Museum and therefore closely involved with debates surrounding the ownership of objects, is adamant that the diversity of the collection should not be undermined by individual interest.

If you follow the logic of returning objects to the place they came from, there would be no international museums

'If you follow the logic of returning objects to the place they came from, there would be no international museums,' he says. 'We would have no way of comparing the achievements of different civilizations. On the other hand, if you guard things too closely at home, it defeats the idea of universal access, and there's no justice in that. Now we're using technology to develop ideas about access, not just through moving objects around the world, but also through the internet. The British Museum can send things all over the world now, and when the objects come home they have accrued another level of history and meaning.'

Equally divisive is the debate surrounding the display of human remains in the British Museum. Again, it concerns issues of ownership, but there are also wider ethical issues about using human remains as objects for public display. A new law governing the treatment of human remains has sparked a debate about the status of this material in museum collections, and the British Museum has been quick to respond by reviewing its collection. The Human Tissue Act 2004 enabled national museums to remove more recent human remains from the collection, and this was the catalyst for a full-scale review of all the Museum's holdings. There are 8663 items in the collection containing human remains, 95 per cent of which are over 1000 years old.

'There are really two issues relating to human remains in the Museum,' says Neil MacGregor. 'Firstly, we have to ask whether something is the actual mortal remains of a person, or if it's been turned into something else, an artefact of some sort. A thigh bone that's been turned into a trumpet is different from a thigh bone that was intended for burial. Secondly, we have to ask if the remains are recent enough to have any emotional link to living people, and if they can be identified. That's when the issue shifts, and the object becomes not a "thing" but a person. And that makes everything different.'

As a result of the first question, all the human remains in the Museum have been reassessed, and some things have been taken off display. 'In the Iron Age gallery, we had a human arm bone with some bangles on it,' says J. D. Hill, curator of the British and European Iron Age collections. 'It was a nineteenth-century find, and when the tomb was excavated the archaeologist left the bangles on the arm bone as he found them. We also had a skull with a crown on it. Both of those items have been removed because we felt that the human remains were not intrinsically interesting, or part of the object in question, but had simply been taken from a body that had been buried. It seems wrong to display part of a body that's come from a whole skeleton. The skull hadn't been taken as a trophy, for instance, in which case it has a different meaning; it was part of a dead person who was properly buried.'

But what about those most famous dead bodies in the Museum, the mummies and the bog bodies? They're hugely popular, and the idea of removing them from display has been thought unthinkable. 'We only display bodies if we think there's an overwhelming educational or intellectual reason for doing so,' says Hill. 'But we do recognize that the majority of our visitors expect us to show them. If we didn't have mummies on display, visitors would be disappointed.'

WAX DEATH MASK OF OLIVER CROMWELL

I like to think that I have the blessed assurance that part of my family fought on the right side in the Civil War. This impression of Oliver Cromwell's face was taken very shortly after his death in 1653; they had to do it quickly, before the features started to fall. Even though my period of specialism is Iron Age Europe, I like a lot of the later objects in the collection – it's nice to step out of your specialism sometimes! People don't always realize that the British Museum has things from recent history as well as the distant past, so this object can come as quite a surprise.

J. D. HILL, *Curator of the British and European Iron Age Collections*

Opposite: Lindow Man, the
first-century AD body found in
a Cheshire peat bog in 1985.
Conditions in the bog meant
that his skin, hair and internal
organs were well preserved.
He was about 25 years old,
his nails were well manicured
and his last meal contained
wheat and barley bread.

Funerary objects, including human remains, are among the main ways by which we learn about ancient cultures; without tombs, there would be no Egyptology, for instance. 'By looking at the dead, we understand how people live,' says Neil MacGregor. 'The burial practices in Ancient Egypt and China preserved information about those civilizations that would otherwise be lost today. We can't be squeamish about it; death and the treatment of the dead are eternal subjects that will always fascinate and trouble mankind.'

But when does a dead body become more than just a dead body? There are no absolute answers. Take the case of Lindow Man, the first-century AD body discovered in a peat bog in northwest England in 1984. He's one of the most popular exhibits in the British Museum's collection, and there's little doubt that visitors would be disappointed if he were removed from display – but, partly because of the extraordinary state of preservation of the body, he is very obviously a dead young man. The conditions in the peat bog mean that we can tell how he died, what he ate before he died, how he cut his hair and finger-nails – so there's no doubt that there are compelling intellectual arguments for the body's display. But we also know that Lindow Man suffered a brutal, gruesome death, struck twice on the top of his head with a heavy object, kicked in the back, strangled with a cord around his neck and then his throat cut. Doesn't the victim of such an atrocity deserve dignity in death? Is that compatible with public display?

He stands for every man and woman in pre-historic Britain. He's the best-preserved ancestor we have

'All the evidence points to a ritual killing,' says J. D. Hill. 'This was not a murder in the sense that we would understand it; this was some kind of human sacrifice. We don't know exactly what the nature of the ritual was, or how this individual came to be the victim – whether he was a criminal who was ritually executed or what. But we must recognize that he is a key cultural icon. He stands for every man and woman in prehistoric Britain. He's the best-preserved ancestor we have. Because he is a real person, he ought to help people connect with the common humanity shared over thousands of years, yet at the same time what we know of his life and death stresses how different people's cultures and beliefs may be to ours.

'The key question we always have to ask is how successfully are we getting visitors to reflect on these issues. What I would like to do is to redesign the display to evoke an atmosphere that is more respectful of him as a human being. I think he should be recognized as a person. We don't put up big neon signs saying, "Lindow Man, This Way!"; we try to keep the atmosphere quite

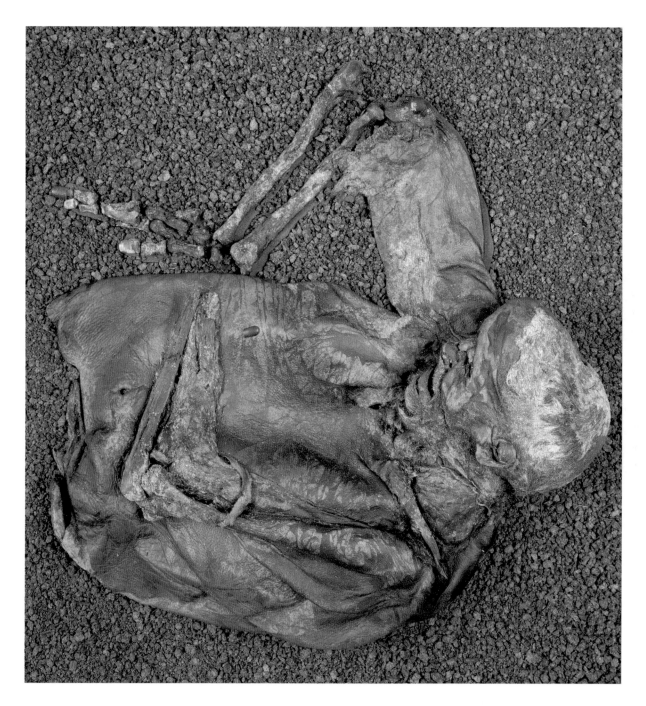

muted, but I think there's more work to be done to create the right context. Visitors are undoubtedly fascinated by him – he's probably the third most-popular display, after the Rosetta stone and the mummies. Obviously, there's a certain amount of gawping. What we have to do is make it easier for visitors to engage with him as a human being. We have to ask questions about murder and ritual killing. People are familiar with those phenomena as part of modern life, and we must help them to relate it to the world of 2000 years ago.'

Above: Two Tasmanian cremation-ash bundles were repatriated in 2006. Here Adam Thompson and Leah Brown from the Tasmanian Aboriginal Centre carry them carefully towards the airport departure gate before the long journey back to their country of origin.

The decision on how to display, if at all, is complex, but lies ultimately in the hands of the British Museum. There are other cases, however, where national and international law must be the deciding factor, and that's when the Museum's board of trustees has to become involved. In 2006, the trustees decided to return two Tasmanian cremation-ash bundles to the Tasmanian Aboriginal Centre, which had long been requesting their repatriation. The move was made possible by a change in the law; the Human Tissue Act, a piece of legislation designed mainly to control the removal, storage and use of human organs by hospitals, contained a section that allowed the British Museum and other institutions to transfer out of the collection human remains that they believed to be less than 1000 years old.

'Before that, there was no way that the British Museum could let go of any of its holdings,' says Baroness Helena Kennedy, the barrister and human rights

IT'S A GREAT HONOUR to be on the board of trustees at the British Museum. I had been the chair of the British Council for six years, so I had connections with the Museum through exhibitions and collections around the world. And I'm a huge admirer of Neil MacGregor, whom I knew when he was at the National Gallery. He's a great curator and a great arts administrator, so I knew it would be wonderful to work with him. When the opportunity to join the board of trustees arose, I applied for it and went through all the proper processes.

I've always loved the British Museum. As a law student in London, I used to go there regularly and use the library. I had a bedsit in Great Russell Street, so it was very much my bit of London, and it became a home from home. When I became a lawyer and started earning money and thinking about getting a mortgage, I bought a flat in Bedford Avenue, which is literally around the corner. I've always used the Museum as a place for reflection; I love to be able to go in and wander around the galleries, just thinking about how other people have lived their lives. It puts the hurly-burly of one's working life in London into perspective.

I'm particularly fond of the Chinese galleries because I find Chinese art very calming. And when my children were small, they were crazy about the mummies, so we spent a lot of time in the Egyptian galleries. One of my greatest discoveries in the British Museum is the print room – it's like a secret garden that nobody knows about. I can ring the bell, and within five minutes I'm sitting down with a Veronese drawing. The fact that you can do that right in the middle of London is something very magical.

HELENA KENNEDY
Trustee of the British Museum

specialist who, as a British Museum trustee, led the debate about the Tasmanian cremation bundles. 'The whole point of leaving something in trust is that subsequent generations can't change the legacy for their own benefit. You're not allowed to interfere with trusts without specific legislative change.'

But the calls for the return of these particular items were becoming pressing. 'The Australian Prime Minister, John Howard, visited Tony Blair here a few years ago,' says Kennedy. 'Howard had been receiving a lot of pressure from the Aboriginal people over things that were being kept in Britain, and Blair and Howard made a joint commitment to get the items returned to them. So a law had to be passed, and the government looked around for the quickest way of doing it. At the time, the Human Tissue Bill was going through Parliament – it was nothing to do with arts or culture, it was a specifically medical piece of legislation. Section 47 was bolted on to it, allowing for the return of human remains to their country of origin. There was a debate in the House of Lords, which I addressed with others, and various amendments were put in to limit it to more recent acquisitions, excluding objects from tombs taken thousands of years ago. But it does allow for the trustees of museums to return human remains in the appropriate circumstances.'

The circumstances in this case could hardly have been more appropriate. The Tasmanian cremation bundles contain ash from human-cremation sites. Relatives of the deceased collected some of the ash and wrapped it in kangaroo skin, keeping the bundle as an amulet against sickness. The bundles were acquired by George Augustus Robinson, who was employed by the colonial government as a 'conciliator' between Tasmanian Aboriginals and Europeans in the 1830s. He travelled around Tasmania from 1829 to 1834, convincing Aborigines to relocate to an off-shore island. His own diaries suggest that he acquired the bundles against the wishes of their owners. They came to the British Museum via the Royal College of Surgeons in 1882.

'This wasn't just a question of someone saying, "We want these things back because they're Australian",' says Kennedy. 'We're talking about human rights, pain and grief and a sense of loss. The Tasmanian Aborigines were victims of genocide. They were practically exterminated, murdered in vast numbers. The descendants of those people are of mixed race. They are understandably angry about what happened to their ancestors. It's not so far in the past; it's only 150 years ago.'

But what can the return of the objects achieve, other than offering a broad gesture of sympathy and regret for the mistakes of the past? 'We had to find out a lot about the funerary practices of the Aboriginal people,' says Kennedy. 'These bundles were taken from the cremation site and were part of the grieving process, and we must regard them as the remains of dead individuals. They rightly belong to the people who claim them, who are an identifiable group of descendants. In this case, the return of the objects allows a process of grieving to be continued, and it acknowledges a period of profound pain for the people of Tasmania who were the victims of an egregious wrong. This was quite a clear-cut case, and it established a protocol that will inform future decisions.'

A special exhibition in the summer of 2006 turned the spotlight on the Warren cup, a first-century AD silver drinking vessel decorated with scenes of men having sex with each other. Nothing could signal more clearly the British Museum's commitment to engaging with its collection in an inquiring way and to confronting issues raised by objects that might once have been swept under the carpet. From the nineteenth century until after the Second World War objects of a sexual nature were kept in the Secretum, a special storage area apart from the rest of the collections. There had been an interest in erotic representations from the ancient world at least since the foundation of the British Museum – but in the nineteenth century, as the collection of sexual material grew, it was deemed unsuitable for public inspection, and hidden away for the exclusive perusal of scholars and clergymen. A large part of the Secretum collection came from George Witt, a nineteenth-century doctor who collected ancient erotica and decided to bequeath it to the Museum rather than encumber his embarrassed family with it. The curious prurience surrounding this part of the Museum's collection began to dissipate in the middle of the twentieth century, as objects were dispersed from the Secretum to their relevant departments.

'Attitudes towards sex were changing,' says Greek and Roman Antiquities Keeper Dyfri Williams, 'and there was no longer a feeling that people had to be protected quite so much. Even so, it took a long time before curators felt comfortable about putting sexual material on open display. In the 1970s, when the Greek and Roman galleries on the ground floor were redone, there was no hesitation about putting out vases with erect penises on them. The shellac was cleaned off, and the vases were revealed in all their splendour.'

> ... it took a long time before curators felt comfortable about putting sexual material on open display

Other objects found their way to the department of Ancient Egypt and the Sudan. 'When the Secretum was dismantled, we got a lot of stuff back,' says Richard Parkinson, assistant Keeper in the department of Ancient Egypt and the Sudan. 'And we have become much bolder. There was a set of wooden phalluses that was excavated in the early twentieth century in Luxor, which had never been displayed until we put them on exhibition in 1999. There were some very funny little figures of men, each wearing his phallus around the neck, like a scarf. Religious iconography in the ancient world is frequently sexually explicit, invoking ideas about fertility. In some ancient Egyptian traditions, the fecundity of the earth god is shown by him engaging in oral masturbation. We put some of these pieces in a temporary exhibition in 1999, but we were still slightly nervous then, and just described them in the exhibition proposal as "votive objects". We had long discussions about how best to display them in a permanent gallery because anything involving ancient Egypt is going to attract school parties. Eventually they went into a case that was all about depictions of

Above: A Roman bronze *tintinabulum* (wind chime) in the form of a winged penis. Phallic amulets like this were often hung in the doorways of Roman houses to protect against evil spirits.

humour and sex; they were contextualized and explained in a non-sensational way. Now I think we're much more confident. I don't think there's anything in the collection that we wouldn't display. The only people who would be shocked are people who have a slightly old-fashioned idea of what a museum is. It's a forum for debate, for public engagement with ideas, not just a static display. The way we present our collection documents changes in ideas.'

But sexually explicit material isn't just out on display in the galleries: it's being actively promoted by exhibitions and events that seek to explore this thorniest of all subjects throughout the Museum. *The Warren Cup: Sex and Society in Ancient Greece and Rome* exhibition brought together artefacts from around the world to contextualize the scenes depicted on the cup itself. It was accompanied by talks examining homosexuality in other ancient cultures.

'The amount of interest generated by that exhibition was extraordinary,' says curator J. D. Hill. 'Anything to do with sex always gets headlines, but this time the press really seemed to engage with the subject in quite an open, interested way. I can't imagine that happening a few years ago. There would have been a lot of nonsense written about how disgusting it was that a national institution was promoting alternative lifestyles, and everyone else would have ignored it. Now it seems that people are willing to engage with a whole range of issues around sex. It's a great example of the British Museum reflecting changes in the broader society. It came around the time of the civil partnership legislation and of films such as *Brokeback Mountain*, which show that we're finally taking a more mature attitude to subjects that have been around since ancient times.'

There are plenty of objects from the ancient world that show same-sex couples in intimate situations, but most of them are open to all sorts of interpretation; there was certainly no fixed concept of sexual preference as we understand it in the twenty-first century. But the Warren cup presents us with two absolutely unambiguous scenes of young men enjoying consensual sex. It's not a mythic scene (no satyrs or gods), it's neither comic nor grotesque, simply documentary and decorative. 'There aren't many pieces in the British Museum's collection that are as challenging as the Warren cup,' says Dyfri Williams, curator of the exhibition and author of a monograph on the object. 'It's completely in your face, and it is a very direct representation of a debate about male sexuality that's been going on for

> It's a great example of the British Museum reflecting changes in the broader society

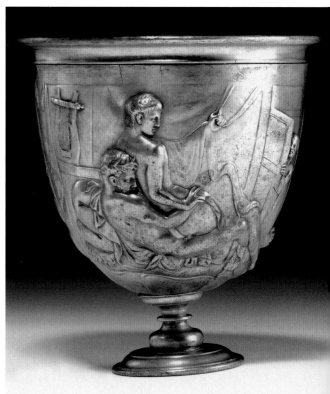

Above: Two views of the Warren cup. On the left a youth makes love to a boy, while on the right a man makes love to a youth, observed by a servant entering through the door at the right.

thousands of years. The modern world isn't static in its ideas about sexuality, so why would the ancient world be?'

Inevitably, the Warren cup's journey to such respectability has been long and tortuous. It was made in the first century AD, probably quite early, possibly during the reign of Augustus. It was a drinking vessel – and would originally have had a pair of handles – for use at banquets, where its decoration would have not only delighted the eye but also stimulated conversation, perhaps about the nature of love, the influence of Greek thought and so on. We do not know who owned it, but we can assume that it was a cultured, wealthy man who was able to afford such high-quality work, and who was sufficiently worldly to regard the subject of male homosexuality as a suitable topic for dinner-party conversation. Judging by the amount of wear on the surface, it appears that the silver was cleaned frequently, suggesting that it remained in regular use for some time.

The Warren cup gained its modern name when it came into the possession of Edward (Ned) Warren, a wealthy American collector, born in 1860, who lived

DYFRI WILLIAMS

Keeper of the Department of Greek and Roman Antiquities

THE KEEPER OF A DEPARTMENT IN THE BRITISH MUSEUM is a mixture of a manager, a curator and, when you can find the time, a scholar. Essentially I run the department, looking after the staff within it and the work they do, and then I have to take an overview of any physical work that needs to be done to the department, the galleries or the collection. Individual curators are responsible for separate bits of the collection, but I'm responsible for all of them. The hardest part of the job is trying to keep up your own research, as the reputation of the Museum rests on the scholarship within it. I have to deal with my subject both nationally and internationally, so it's important to find the time to devote to research, even though it's not easy.

I've been here for 27 years – it's a life sentence! People do tend to work in the curatorial departments for a long time; it's a matter of having a passion for the objects, and this really is a great collection. To move anywhere else, you'd have to have a very specific reason for doing so.

This is one of the top four collections of Greek and Roman antiquities in the world. Our real strength is in the sculpture, and we have very good vases and jewellery. The collection is very important in isolation because the artefacts of Ancient Greece and Rome tell us about the emergence of Western civilization, but the wonderful thing about the British Museum is that we can look at them in the context of other world civilizations. That helps us to see not just what's important about the Greek and Roman collection, but also what's good about other things.

People have this idea that the British Museum is full of dusty boxes in the cellars, but that's really not true. Since the 1980s we've tried to get as much on show as possible. What were storage spaces were turned into the basement galleries, and we've packed them with material. The creation of the Enlightenment Gallery has also allowed us to get more objects on show in a different context, and it's a delight to see those things next to objects from completely different places.

My particular interest is Greek vases; I came here as a specialist in that area, and it remains my great love. They're beautiful objects, but they tell us so much about the development of Western culture. And we have one of the best collections in the world – so why would I go anywhere else?

with his companion John Marshall at Lewes House in Lewes, East Sussex. Warren was passionate about classical antiquities, which he collected avidly; he also used the family fortune to acquire such treasures as Rodin's *The Kiss* (which he actually commissioned) and Cranach's *Adam and Eve*. Warren acquired the cup in 1911 on a buying trip in Rome; the dealer who sold it to him supplied the information that it had been found at Bittir, 10 km from Jerusalem, with coins from the reign of Claudius. It is possible that the cup had been taken from Rome to Judaea by a wealthy Roman official, who then left in a hurry during the Jewish Revolt against Rome of AD 66–74, leaving his possessions hidden for later collection – which never happened.

Exactly when the cup was found isn't known, but its history after 1911, when it entered Warren's collection, is well documented. Warren treasured it – there are reports that his friends called it 'the Holy Grail' – as an important relic of homosexual love in the ancient world. When he died in 1928, the cup was left to Harold Thomas, his secretary. Thomas tried, and failed, to sell the cup, and kept it hidden away in his attic until 1952, when it was sent to a collector in New York. Fate intervened in the shape of an Italian Catholic customs official, who inspected the cup, decided it was pornographic and had it sent back to England. By this time Thomas had died, and his widow sold it to a British dealer, John K. Hewett, who offered it to the British Museum.

Above: The acquisition of the Warren cup in 1999 caused a flurry of interest, inspiring cartoons like this one by Nick Newman for the *Sunday Times*. It was even mentioned on the television comedy quiz *Have I Got News for You?*

This first approach to the British Museum failed. The trustees would not even consider the offer – and, as the chairman of the trustees was the Archbishop of Canterbury, they may have had a point. The cup wandered around various collectors and institutions, none of whom was brave enough to buy it. Eventually, in 1966, Hewett sold the cup to a private collector abroad. That might have been the end of the story, but in 1992 the owner, sensing a change in public attitudes, put the cup on display in Basel and then in the Metropolitan Museum of Art in New York. In 1998 it was sold to a British collector and once again offered to the British Museum.

'This time we got in fast,' says Dyfri Williams. 'We knew that it had been offered to us about 40 years before, and we'd missed out on it that time. I did not want that to happen again. Of course, we didn't have the money to buy it outright ourselves, so I went to the Heritage Lottery Fund, making a strong case for the importance of the piece. The Museum acquired it in 1999, and it's now one of the stars of our collection.'

RED-FIGURED WINE COOLER

This is a good example of a piece that used to be hidden away from public view. It's a wine cooler, made in Athens around 500 BC and signed by the great painter Douris: you fill it with wine and then set it in a large bowl filled with ice-cold water till the wine is cool. The decoration shows satyrs, who were followers of the wine god Dionysos, doing various tricks involving wine cups. One of them is balancing a cup on the end of his erect penis. At some point in the nineteenth century the penis was painted out with black shellac so that it looked as if the cup were floating in the air! When it went into the newly refurbished, post-Second World War galleries, however, the shellac was cleaned off, and suddenly the scene made sense again.

DYFRI WILLIAMS, *Keeper of the Department of Greek and Roman Antiquities*

The history of the Warren cup offers a direct challenge to the idea that the history of human civilization is one of steady progress and enlightenment. In the first century AD there were artists and collectors who were sophisticated and liberal enough to consider the Warren cup a suitable object for their attention. Nearly 2000 years later it found a home in a similarly civilized enclave in Sussex, where Ned Warren and his friends attempted to live according to the high ideals of platonic love. But as soon as the cup was thrown on the stormy waters of the twentieth century, it encountered every modern manifestation of prurience, censorship, prejudice and cowardice that could be imagined. Times finally changed enough to allow it a moment of glory in the British Museum – but they could easily change again.

'Ideas about sexuality and the acceptability of certain kinds of sexual behaviour are culturally determined,' says Neil MacGregor. 'Attitudes change and fluctuate through the centuries, even through the decades. The Warren cup hasn't changed much in 2000 years, but attitudes towards it change all the time. Sexuality is as much a matter of debate now as it was for the wealthy Romans who created the cup. When we put the exhibition together, we deliberately included a still from the film *Brokeback Mountain* to show that the world is still struggling with the same issues that exercised our ancestors. It's important for the Museum to assert that whatever position our society takes on this question, other societies have taken different ones. Human behaviour is a constant: basically, people have been doing the same things together throughout history. It's attitudes and cultures that change.'

8

A museum for everyone

The British Museum is a London landmark, a tourist magnet and a resource for the nation. Beyond British shores, however, it enjoys an equal, if not higher, reputation as a guardian and sponsor of the world's cultural heritage – and it's this global aspect to the Museum's work, increasingly facilitated by transport and communications technology, that is coming to predominate in the twenty-first century. Pursuing eighteenth-century concepts of universal access to their logical ends means making the collection as available as possible to the citizens of the world – and if that means taking the BM's treasures out on the road, that's what will be done. But there's another reason for the constant re-evaluation of the British Museum's relationship with world cultures, as an already diverse British cultural and ethnic mix continues to evolve with the arrival and integration of new people – and audiences – from around the world.

'I had a conversation with the Department for Culture, Media and Sport recently,' says director Neil MacGregor, 'in which I was trying to explore with them the role that the British Museum plays in the social cohesion of this country. In 2006 we had a wide range of public debates, including one about the meaning of the Crucifixion, related to drawings in our collection by Michelangelo and Rembrandt. We had discussions about Islamic theology connected to the *Word into Art* exhibition of Middle Eastern work. And we had a season of events celebrating Bengali culture, with input from Hindus and Muslims. A series of public debates, organized in association with the *Guardian* and chaired by the broadcaster and journalist Jon Snow, have also ranged over contemporary issues from Sudan to Iraq, and sought to set them within the historical and cultural context provided by the Museum's collection.' The British Museum is one of the very few public spaces where all these things could occur, where everyone has an equal stake in the world's culture, whatever their national, religious or ethnic background.

The world gathers under the roof of the British Museum, not just culturally, but also demographically. The Africa season of 2005 culminated in a day that saw 25,000 visitors pass through the doors, many of them people from the African diaspora who had not seen the collection before. The 2006 *Voices of Bengal* season was focused on a huge tableau of the Hindu goddess Durga, built on site by Bengali craftsmen and subsequently taken to the nearby

Above: Children working on a special task during a Museum sleepover event. Opposite: An early stage in creating the Durga in the Great Court.

Camden Centre. These are just two examples of Museum projects that bring diverse audiences into the building, and acknowledge, explore and celebrate the tapestry of cultural influences that make up modern Britain.

It's not just audiences that meet at the British Museum; it's also become the arena for some unlikely diplomatic advances that could only happen under the umbrella of politically neutral scholarship. At the 2005 opening of the *Forgotten Empire* exhibition, a celebration of the fabulous riches of ancient Persia, the then foreign secretary Jack Straw and Iranian vice-president Esfandiyar Rahim Mashayi came together at a time when political relations between the two countries were, to say the least, strained. The 2006 *Word into Art* exhibition drew the spotlight away from the inflammatory debate about Danish cartoons and on to a tradition of sacred and secular Middle Eastern art that transcended the hysteria of newspaper reports. In 2000 the Museum's new Korean Gallery was opened, and, in 2001, official representatives from both sides of the demarcation line between North and South Korea, the 38th parallel, had a rare meeting at the reception for an exhibition of North Korean contemporary art and a Korean study day.

'It was a diplomatic minefield,' says Jane Portal, curator of the Chinese and Korean collections. 'We'd been very carefully setting up relations with the communist government in North Korea, and when their representatives were visiting the Museum we were also welcoming the ambassador from South Korea. Officials from the North and South tend not to run into each other; it could only happen at an event like that, where they're united by a cultural history that goes way back before the division. Cultural artefacts will always transcend the politics of the day. They speak about the eternal qualities.'

> **Cultural artefacts will always transcend the politics of the day. They speak about the eternal qualities**

The British Museum's traffic with the wider world is very much two-way. Objects come into the Museum to be shown in exhibitions; objects are loaned by the Museum to museums in other countries. There's also a sharing of knowledge and skills. Curators and conservators criss-cross the globe to and from the British Museum, exchanging information and techniques that add immeasurably to the understanding and preservation of cultural artefacts. Experts in Chinese scroll painting have come to London for a three-year project at the British Museum, helping to read the collection and produce an online catalogue. In exchange, two clock curators travelled to the Palace Museum in Beijing, where they discussed methods of conservation and documentation with the resident clock experts. As it

I STUDIED CHINESE AT CAMBRIDGE in the 1970s; I was originally going to do French, but then I changed my mind. A lot of people thought it a really weird choice – my teachers thought I was mad and tried hard to dissuade me. But I had an idea that Chinese was going to be a very important language in the future, and there weren't that many people studying it in those days, so I sensed I might have a better chance of achieving something in a smaller field. In retrospect, it's the best decision I ever made, but it was pretty scary at the time. I had to start completely from scratch. Even when I graduated, I couldn't actually speak a word of Chinese because the powers that be at Cambridge decided that we should learn classical Chinese, which is a dead language. I was able to read Tang poetry, but I couldn't actually order a coffee on my first trip to Beijing.

After graduation, I studied archaeology at Beijing University; I was the first woman from outside China to do that. I made a lot of good friends and contacts at that time, and the people I knew as students then are now high up in the Ministry of Culture or the universities, which is quite handy. Organizing international relations with museums is all about building up relationships, and it's been really useful for me. The first time I went to China with Neil MacGregor, we sat down at an official meeting and a couple of people from the ministry came over and said, 'I don't suppose you remember us, but we were in the same class as you.'

I started at the British Museum in 1987, initially working on Chinese material. Since then I've also taken on the Korean collection, which entailed learning Korean. I have to do an awful lot of travelling. In 2005 I went out to the Far East eight times.

JANE PORTAL

Curator of the Chinese
and Korean Collections

represents the cultures of the world, the British Museum has links with every part of the world. Objects and resources are shared wherever they are needed: a U'mista mask made by the Kwakwaka'wakw people has recently been loaned to the U'mista Cultural Centre in British Columbia, allowing a key cultural artefact of Canadian first-nation people to remain as a catalyst for further developments in that area. But, despite the global demand, the British Museum has limited resources, both financially and academically, which it has to shepherd in order to have any significant impact.

The Museum's main overseas focus is now threefold, with special strategies in place to develop relationships with Africa, China and the Middle East. Until 1998 much of the African collection, now forming part of the department of Africa, Oceania and the Americas, was housed separately in the

THE ADMONITIONS SCROLL

The Admonitions Scroll *is the world's most famous Chinese painting. It's a painted hand-scroll from the sixth century* AD, *illustrating a third-century text about how to be an ideal concubine to the emperor – and it's a veiled criticism of the empress of the time, who was far from ideal. It's very long and incredibly fragile, with beautifully written text interspersed with illustrations attributed to Gu Kaizhi, a very famous figure painter. Its history is very interesting: it was collected by various different emperors, who all left their seals on it, including the Qianlong emperor in the eighteenth century, who declared it to be one of the four great beauties in his collection. It's not on permanent display because it's so fragile – we can only have it out for three months of the year – but there's a CD of it, and it is on the BM website, so it's always available for study.*

JANE PORTAL, *Curator of the Chinese and Korean Collections*

Museum of Mankind. That collection returned to Bloomsbury and now has its own gallery – and it's been identified as an area of the Museum's collection that needs particular development, both in terms of acquisition and research. China is emerging from a long period of cultural isolation, and the British Museum has been at the forefront of attempts to forge links with the West that will give everyone a chance to share a massive and little-known cultural heritage, while offering to the Chinese people a chance to see treasures that we in the West have long taken for granted. And the Middle East, always a focus of BM activity since the eighteenth century, continues to yield extraordinary treasures. It's also an area that calls on all the diplomatic strengths of the Museum, as the shifting political situation causes problems of access and endangers the collections of those volatile countries (see pages 176–83).

All three international strategies are based on Memoranda of Understanding agreed between the British Museum and various governmental and non-governmental organizations in the relevant countries. In Africa there are Memoranda of Understanding with Kenya, Ethiopia, Mali, Ghana, Mozambique and Zimbabwe, as well as with the West African Museums Programme, based in Senegal and working with museums in 16 countries. Claude Ardouin, head of the Museum's African section, coordinates and supervises the BM's Africa programme.

'The African Partnership Programme has been a major development of the last few years,' he says. 'When I joined the British Museum in 2005, it was in its starting phase, but it's come a long way since then, and it's now reaching maturity. We've developed good working partnerships with heritage institutes in Africa, targeting the exchange of skills, information and collections. This helps us to share our collection, our experience and know-how with our partners in Africa, and it also brings in to the British Museum a great deal of

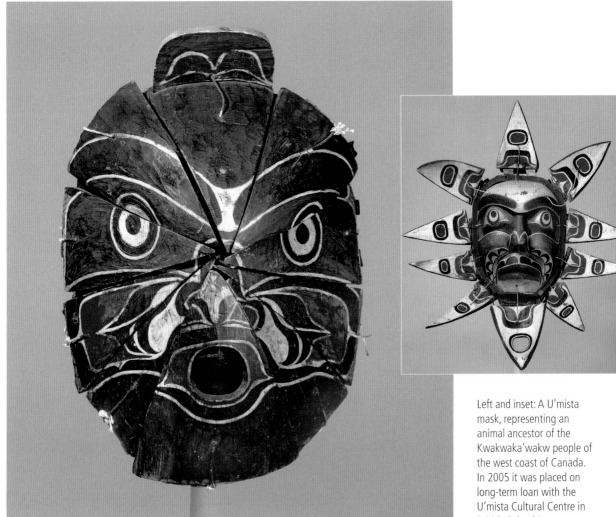

Left and inset: A U'mista mask, representing an animal ancestor of the Kwakwaka'wakw people of the west coast of Canada. In 2005 it was placed on long-term loan with the U'mista Cultural Centre in British Columbia.

new knowledge and understanding that helps us better address our collections, our interpretation and our diaspora audiences in the UK. The African diaspora is a major component in the UK now, in a way that it wasn't 20 years ago, and the BM must respond to that. Through this partnership we also contribute to strengthen the capacities and the professional skills of the partner institutions through training and advice. In the UK the University of East Anglia (UEA) and London's Horniman Museum are our major partners in this African Partnership Programme, and we do hope that in the near future other UK institutions will join us.'

CLAUDE ARDOUIN

Head of the African Section

I WAS BORN AND GREW UP IN MALI, and my family still lives there. I started my career in museums as the director of the National Museum of Mali from 1981 to 1987, then became executive director of the West African Museums Programme in Dakar, Senegal. I came to the British Museum in 2005, and it was a big move – but it was an opportunity I just couldn't turn down. The British Museum itself *is* the heritage of the world: that's how it's regarded in Africa, and that's how I still regard it. To work in that environment is very appealing, and I don't know anyone in my field who would resist. I'm certainly planning to stay for a while.

I've been doing a lot of travelling to and from Africa since I've been based here in London. Partly, I'm developing partnerships with other heritage institutions, finalizing Memoranda of Understanding, doing work with the universities, planning loans and exhibitions. But I also have my own field research to do. I've just started the research for a major project about the history of gold in West Africa, so I spent a lot of time with two old goldsmiths in Dakar, looking at their techniques and traditions.

It's very interesting for me to watch the black and African diaspora audience growing at the British Museum. A lot of African groups are coming in now, not just to see the Africa Gallery, but also to explore the rest of the BM's collection. My office overlooks the forecourt, so I get a good, at-a-glance idea of how many African groups are coming in, and it's really growing. Since the big Africa season in 2005, people who had never been before are coming back and bringing their friends. It's a new audience for the BM, and one that I'm very happy to develop.

A good example of this two-way traffic is the 2006 *Hazina* exhibition in the National Museums of Kenya, Nairobi. *Hazina* means 'treasures' in Kiswahili, and the exhibition brings together objects from Kenyan national collections, as well as a significant loan of 150 objects from the British Museum – the first time the BM has loaned objects to sub-Saharan Africa. 'It's not just a straightforward loan,' says Ardouin. 'The lead curator from Kenya, Kiprop Lagat, came to the UK to do a master's at UEA, and then worked on our African collection, choosing the objects he wanted to take back to Kenya. He designed the concept of the exhibition, which then became a multi-disciplinary project involving design, interpretation, conservation and marketing. The whole team came over here twice to train with our specialist departments. When the exhibition opened in Nairobi in 2006, it had a massive impact. I think there was real pleasure that the British Museum was working with Kenya in this way, and it opened people's eyes to a different aspect of their cultures. The cultural view in Africa tends to be defined by contemporary political frontiers and ethnic boundaries – but *Hazina* showed a heritage of trading and interaction among different groups over many centuries. It's a completely new way of looking at the whole of East Africa as a cultural area, not just country by country or people by people.'

In return, the African collection at the British Museum benefited from the attention of the Kenyan team. 'Kiprop Lagat brought a lot of new material to the interpretation of our collection,' says Ardouin. 'Sometimes it's necessary to see an object through the eyes of the people who made it or whose ancestors made it. Whenever something goes out of the British Museum on loan, it always returns with its meaning greatly enriched.'

After 2005's Africa season at the British Museum, highlighting treasures from the African collection, such as the stone tools from Olduvai Gorge in Tanzania, and the success of the *Hazina* exhibition in Kenya, the Africa project looks set to go from strength to strength. Forthcoming partnership ventures will celebrate the fiftieth anniversary of the independence of Ghana, and Ardouin is just beginning the research phase of a major research and exhibition project looking at the role that gold played in the history of West Africa. But the project that's likely to get the biggest headlines in 2007 is *Atlantic Trade and Identity*, a programme of events designed to mark the 200 years since a parliamentary Act was passed to abolish the slave trade in the then British Empire. The British Museum will host an installation by Benin artist Romuald Hazoumé entitled *La Bouche du Roi*, a huge re-creation of the slave ship *The Brookes*, using plastic petrol cans and mixed media to represent the commodification of human beings. Meanwhile, an exhibition by the BM's department of Coins and

BRONZE HEAD WITH BEADED CROWN AND PLUME

This fascinating object comes from the ancient city state of Ile-Ife in Nigeria and was probably made some time in the twelfth to fourteenth centuries AD, but we still know very little about it. It is believed to represent the Oni, the King of Ife, wearing a beaded crown. Ife is the place where, according to Yoruba tradition, the gods came down from heaven to populate the world. What's really impressive about this head is the degree of sophistication in the expression and the realism of the whole work.

When the first brass head was discovered in the early twentieth century, it was assumed to have been produced by a non-African civilization, as it was believed that African artists had never had such expertise, but research has now revealed to the world some stunning aspects of the history and creativity of West African societies during the twelfth century. It is interesting to see how these ancient works now influence the contemporary creativity at Ile-Ife. It's a piece of art that remains very much alive and strong, and it is certainly one of our best African masterpieces.

CLAUDE ARDOUIN, *Head of the African Section*

Right: *La Bouche du Roi*, a huge artwork by Benin artist Romuald Hazoumé, created at the British Museum in 2007.

Medals will also explore the trade in slaves and the money that was made from it.

The British Museum's China strategy has already led to major loans, and is about to bear fruit with the arrival of the massive *First Emperor* exhibition in September 2007, bringing some of the famous terracotta army to the UK. Again, the entire China project is based on a mixture of diplomacy and political strategy in which cultural considerations are paramount. 'We've been going to China quite a lot,' says Jane Portal, senior Chinese curator in the department of Asia and holder of the China strategy. 'Neil MacGregor first came over with me in 2004 for a lot of preliminary discussions with the various museums and representatives from the Ministry of Culture; then, in September 2005, we signed the Memorandum of Understanding (MOU) in the Great Hall of the People in Beijing, in the presence of Tony Blair and the Chinese premier Wen Jiabao. The MOU guarantees a significant programme of collaboration between the British Museum and its Chinese counterparts. Since then we've signed MOUs with other museums, including the Palace Museum in the Forbidden City.'

Above: The British prime minister and the Chinese premier at the signing of the Memorandum of Understanding in Beijing.

Signing the memoranda isn't just a simple question of putting a mark on a piece of paper; there were several banquets to be enjoyed before and after. 'There are always a lot of toasts to be drunk,' says Portal. 'When we signed the MOU at the Palace Museum, Neil and I were taken up to an official government hostelry called the Fishing Terrace, where the emperor used to stop on his way to the summer palace. It's a very snazzy place, and they laid on a banquet there for about 15 of us to discuss our future plans. They gave us course after course after course; the food just kept on coming. Some of it was delicious; some of it was just very strange. There was a dish called "The Monk Jumped over the Wall" – supposedly because the food on the other side was so delicious – which tasted like a mixture of fish and beef, not to my liking. At another banquet, in Xi'an, they served a lot of *baijiu*, a distilled spirit that is very, very strong, and we had to drink to seal the relationship. I was certainly feeling a little weary the next day.'

The first fruits of this new cultural relationship between Britain and China was a major exhibition in the Capital Museum in Beijing, entitled *Treasures of the World's Cultures*, comprising 272 objects from the British Museum collection, including handaxes from the Olduvai Gorge, Egyptian mummies, Greek busts and Roman sculpture. Later, in 2006, a huge loan of objects went to Shanghai for the *Assyria: Art and Empire* exhibition.

We've sent them some of our greatest treasures, and in return London will get to see the terracotta warriors

'Before the signing of the memoranda, we had a rather piecemeal relationship with China,' say Portal. 'We have sent things there before: in 1999 we sent over a big Egyptian show, which was seen by nearly 630,000 people. But we didn't follow it up, and the impetus was lost. Now we've got a plan in place, and it means we'll get a lot more mutual sharing of collections and expertise. The *Assyria* exhibition got an amazing reaction in Shanghai; you have to remember that they just haven't seen this material in China – it's been closed off for such a long time. Because of economic developments, people in China are now hungry for world culture in a way that they have never been before. They've started travelling outside China a bit more now, but the best way for them to see the cultures of the world is if they come to them. And now, for the first time in a long time, they're willing to share their own cultural treasures with the rest of the world. There is so much good stuff in the national and provincial museums in China, and it doesn't get seen. That's changing now, and we can take advantage of that.'

'It's a quid pro quo arrangement,' says Neil MacGregor. 'Our lending to

Above: Neil MacGregor and Jane Portal looking at the terracotta warriors at the on-site museum in Xi'an.

them makes it easier, politically, for them to lend to us. We've sent them some of our greatest treasures, and the huge Assyrian exhibition, and in return London will get to see the terracotta warriors. It's a delicate bit of cultural diplomacy involving many papers and many official stamps and lots of eating and drinking, but in the end everyone benefits.'

British audiences will see the benefits of this burgeoning cultural relationship with the arrival in 2007 of the *First Emperor* exhibition, a massive loan from Xi'an in Shaanxi province. 'We'll be getting a lot of the famous terracotta figures,' says Portal. 'We've been to see them, and they're really wonderful; they're going to make a tremendous impact. Not just terracotta warriors but also terracotta bureaucrats, acrobats, animals and birds – all the things that the emperor would need to serve him in the afterlife. The site in Xi'an was discovered in 1974, and it still hasn't been fully excavated. There's a mound in the middle, which we think contains the tomb of the emperor Qin Shihuangdi (the First Emperor), but no digging has been done yet. It's said that there's a whole city of the dead under there, with rivers of mercury, stars made of precious stones in the ceiling, a depiction of the whole universe. We're not just designing an exhibition that shows artefacts from the tomb site; we're also telling the story of the emperor himself and of how he unified China in the third century BC. We hope the exhibition will have the same kind of impact as Tutankhamun did in the seventies, and enthuse a whole generation of schoolchildren. We'd like to see far more schools studying ancient China. It's just as fascinating and just as glamorous as Egypt. This is the man who built the Great Wall of China, after all. That's as good as the pyramids any day.'

ending precious ancient objects around the world is all very well in theory, but in reality it's a massive operation fraught with practical and official difficulties. Before any loan is considered, the British Museum has to be certain that the destination museum can provide the right conditions and security. 'We can only lend responsibly,' says Neil MacGregor. 'The museums we're sending objects to have to be able to ensure their safety. Beijing now has a museum that can accept international loans: it's new, and it reaches international standards, and it's very pleasing that they chose to open it with an exhibition of British Museum treasures. Shanghai, being a more cosmopolitan city, has had a good museum for a long time – and there are places opening up in the Chinese provinces that we'll be happy to work with. It's easier and safer to transport these big, valuable objects now – but it's just as important to be certain that they'll be safe at the other end.'

The people responsible for making sure that loan objects get to their destination in one piece are a team drawn from the Museum assistants, the BM's stage hands, as it were, who are responsible for all the physical handling of the collection. Nic Lee is head of the Stone, Wall Paintings and Mosaics Conservation section, and with him begins the responsibility of getting large lumps of rock from their home in London to places all over the world. He and his team worked on the *Assyria: Art and Empire* exhibition that went to Shanghai in 2006, taking 251 objects – many of them large, all of them priceless – to the other side of the world.

'The process starts in the Conservation department,' says Lee. 'Whenever there's a request for a loan, we have to inspect the object and declare that it's fit for purpose. What condition is the object in? Can it be safely moved? If there's going to be a possibility that it will suffer during transit, we'll do a conservation treatment that ensures the object's durability. And there are cosmetic treatments to make it look good, up to exhibition standard.'

CRADLE TO GRAVE BY PHARMACOPOEIA

I think Cradle to Grave *is one of the most exciting pieces in the Museum at the moment. It consists of two huge lengths of fabric, with thousands of pills incorporated into it to represent all the medication that we might take during a lifetime. Along the way, it tells stories about births, marriages and deaths, about illnesses that we might have in our lifetime – I just think it's a really provocative and fresh way of looking at life. Every time I walk through the Wellcome Trust Gallery, there are people crowding around it, moving very slowly, taking in the story; it seems to grab people in a way that some other things don't.*

NIC LEE, *Head of the Stone, Wall Paintings and Mosaics Conservation Section*

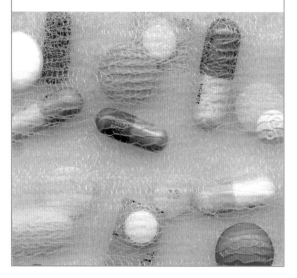

Once Conservation has given the go-ahead, they work in conjunction with Darrel Day, who rejoices in the job title of senior heavy-objects handler. 'I started at the British Museum as a mason's assistant, moving heavy objects in the Greek and Roman collection,' he says. 'Then I went to the Egyptian department as a museum assistant, then became a senior museum assistant – so I've had a lot of experience of moving heavy things around the Museum and around the world. This new job enables me to work across all the collections. If it's big and heavy, I'm responsible for it, whether it's moving three feet across the gallery floor or all the way to China.'

> I've had a lot of experience of moving heavy things around … If it's big and heavy, I'm responsible

There were some specific challenges in the *Assyria: Art and Empire* exhibition. These were not simply statues that could be picked up on a forklift, crated up and shipped. Many of the biggest, most famous objects were attached to the walls of the British Museum and had to be taken off before they could go anywhere. 'The Nimrud Palace wall reliefs are mounted on brackets that are fixed to the wall, then the brackets are covered over with plaster for display purposes,' says Day. 'So first of all we have to cut away the plaster, then extract the reliefs from the wall, remove the brackets and get the objects on to a forklift truck. They go straight on to what we call a module – an L-shape stand made of MDF and pine – that holds and supports them, so you can forklift them without actually touching them. The reliefs are made of alabaster, which scratches very easily, so you need to minimize the amount of handling. They stay on those modules until they come back home.' For the Assyrian loan, 24 objects were big enough to need modules.

The panels, safely mounted, are then packed up. Packaging methods and materials are determined by the size and shape of the object, but generally speaking they're covered in special acid-free conservation tissue, then fitted with a foam shell and packed in a wooden crate. Once packed, they have to be taken out of the Museum and loaded on to a plane. 'The British Museum is a very old building,' says Day, 'so it doesn't have any purpose-built loading facilities. We have to forklift the crates out of the building and then get them up on to a truck trailer; then they're safe to be driven to the airport. If an object's not too big, it can go on a regular flight – but the Assyrian reliefs are so big and heavy that they can only go in a cargo plane. The only flight we could find, with the right plane and the right insurance coverage, was in Luxembourg, so we had to truck the crates there first, before putting them on an 11-hour flight that stopped over in Azerbaijan and then went on to Shanghai.'

Right: Installing the huge wall panels for the Assyrian exhibition in China.

The crates are carefully labelled and numbered, and handed over to specialist loading staff at the airports. 'That's the only part of the process that we can't do ourselves, for security reasons. We're not allowed on to the tarmac, so it has to be done by the shipping company. But we have good procedures in place to make sure the crates are safe; they're all netted and wrapped up in polythene. We were shipping this stuff out in May 2006, just before the World Cup, so all the numbers on the crates corresponded to the numbers in the England squad. Crate number seven had a Beckham shirt; number eight – which was an enormous genie – was Lampard. It lightened the mood a bit, and we were really surprised when we got to China to discover that they knew all about David Beckham!'

Two aeroplanes carried the entire exhibition plus the BM team of seven that accompanied it They landed in the very early hours of the morning and had to work through the day to get the crates safely from the airport to the museum. 'The museum in Shanghai is a new building, but it's got low doorways,' says Day. 'They've got a purpose-built loading ramp, which is great, but some of the crates just wouldn't go in. The lift wasn't big enough for the biggest objects, so they had to be rolled in through the front door – which meant we had to get a mobile crane to get them up the steps. Even then we had to unpack three of the modules to get a bit more clearance. And finally there was the genie – or Lampard as he was known – who was still too tall, so we had to lay him down on his side. We knew that before we went, so we'd packed it in such a way that it could be safely placed in a horizontal position.'

Once inside, the crates were unpacked and the objects carefully checked by curators and conservators to make sure they'd survived the journey. 'There were a few little conservation things that I had to do,' says Nic Lee, 'but they'd all travelled well. A bit of support broke off one of the reliefs, but that was a bit of nineteenth-century restoration that I'd been wanting to get rid of for ages anyway.' Once they'd got a clean bill of health, the objects were installed in their designated display areas – in some cases placed directly into holes on the wall, still sitting on their modules. This done, the designers moved in to complete the exhibition, and the countdown began for the grand opening ceremony.

'The press were there in force, and it was good to see so much excitement and so many people coming to see the objects,' says Darrel Day. 'It gives you the satisfaction of a job well done. But my main interest is knowing that they're safely installed until we go back and take them off the walls and do the whole process in reverse.'

The loan of Assyrian objects to China was one of the biggest international moves in recent years – but, at any given time, large objects from the British Museum collection are moving around various parts of the world, constantly supervised by teams of curators, conservators and museum assistants who go with them every step of the way. 'Loans make up the biggest single part of my job,' says Evan York, senior museum assistant in the department of Ancient Egypt and the Sudan. 'Some things are pretty straightforward to pack up and move, like the big, blocky sculptures or stelae. But other things are a real challenge. The worst things to

HEAD OF A STATUE OF AMENHOTEP III

It's hard to choose one favourite object because they're all so special. But the one that I have the most feeling for is the Amenhotep head because I've taken it all over the world. It was one of the earliest pieces I moved; I've taken it to India and all across the USA and Canada. Every so often I have to fly out somewhere and move it on, so I've got to know it pretty well over the years. It's a very nice piece of stone, with some good markings in the quartzite, and it's very cleverly carved so that the features really stand out.

DARREL DAY, *Senior Heavy-objects Handler*

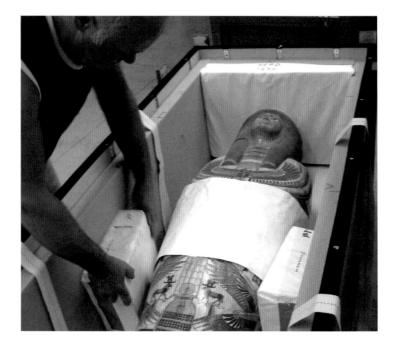

pack are the tomb models – large, very delicate replicas of boats and scenes from daily life. The model boats can be about a metre long, with cloth sails and rigging and lots of little figures, all painted. You can't dismantle them and reassemble them at the other end. They're made of wood and organic materials, so they have the potential to be easily damaged. They're not really meant to be moved much at all – they were designed to sit in the tomb for ever, and the only journey they'd make was to the afterlife. Sometimes we have to make a judgement that an object is just too fragile to travel, that it can't be packed and moved safely. But, generally, we do what we can to make them safe to move.'

Egyptian objects are, of course, among the most requested items from the British Museum collection, and they take Evan York and his team all over the world. 'There's a touring exhibition of large Egyptian sculpture that's been going around the US and Canada for over five years, and we have to supervise each and every move. Then there's the *Mummy: the Inside Story* exhibition, which started here at the British Museum in 2005, and has since travelled to two museums in

I DID A SPORTS SCIENCE DEGREE AT UNIVERSITY, and played semi-pro basketball, so museum work wasn't exactly what I had in mind when I started out. But after graduating I decided I didn't want a career in sports, and I'd always been interested in archaeology and Egyptology, so I got myself a job in the British Museum and ended up working in the accounts department for two years. I was just waiting for an opening in the Egypt department to come up – and as soon as it did, I applied.

The job of museum assistant is a tricky one to recruit for. It's not really got much to do with what you've done in your career so far; it's more to do with a state of mind, an attitude and an aptitude for the job. It's really about common sense more than anything; the rest you can learn. I got a temporary contract, then I worked as a museum assistant for over seven years before being promoted to senior museum assistant, which means I manage a team of four. One of us has to look after the study room every day, which leaves the rest of us to do all the physical work on the collection. That involves preparing things for loans and actually taking them to their destination, as well as a huge amount of other things within the Museum. There are storage areas that need refurbishing; so we've got to move tens of thousands of pieces. And if anything needs moving across a gallery floor, that's our job. If something goes into Conservation, we have to get it there and move it about as required. We've done a lot of shifting of the Nebamun wall paintings for Conservation over the last few years. If someone wants to see an object for research or photography, we have to get it there. There's never a dull moment.

EVAN YORK

Senior Museum Assistant, Department of Ancient Egypt and the Sudan

Being physically strong obviously helps in this job, but it's not essential. I would never dream of just picking something up with brute force, even if I could; you have to do things the right way, to protect the object and the people around it. We just do things carefully, slowly and safely. Sometimes we use the most old-fashioned methods, driving a little wedge of wood underneath a large object, then another on the other side, gradually rocking it up until it's at the level we want. That's usually how they would have moved large things when the Museum opened in the eighteenth century, and it's probably how they would have done it thousands of years ago. Often, nowadays, we need things done quickly, so we get them up on a forklift, but it's not always necessary. There's something satisfying about using the old methods; it puts you closer to the history of the objects and the people who found them.

Most of my work is very practical, which I like, but I've also taken the opportunity to develop my knowledge and understanding of ancient Egyptian culture. While I was working in the accounts department, I did a certificate in archaeology at night school, then took a degree in Egyptology and then a master's degree. I haven't quite finished it; I had to defer writing my dissertation because I now have a two-year-old son, so I don't have a lot of time to devote to study in the evenings!

I still get a real buzz from being around the collection. It's not so much handling the objects – I don't have that kind of cavalier attitude of treating them as my own toys to play with. I really enjoy the chance to look at them, to learn how they were made, to understand the art, the craftsmanship, how they were used and their place in a cultural context. That's something I'd find very hard to give up.

Page 162: Egyptian objects
are among the most
requested items from the
British Museum's collection,
and they take Evan York and
his team all over the world.
Right: Evan York prepares to
move the head of Ramesses II
to its new position.

the US and now to Japan, getting a bit bigger each time. The Japanese
audience is very interested in Egypt, so we've added more coffins, mummies
and funerary equipment and related objects.'

York's credo for his job is simple: 'I want things to come back here in the
same state as they left. That's what we strive to achieve. The only way to
protect an object absolutely is to keep it in a store cupboard, not even in a
gallery. But then what's the point of having the object? We have a duty to let
the world see this material, and it's our job to strike a balance between
maximum access and reasonable safety.'

9

A virtual space for the twenty-first century

A virtual space for the twenty-first century

The British Museum has endured for over 250 years. It has survived the Gordon riots in 1780, thanks to 600 soldiers being sent to protect the Museum from the destructive mobs. It has survived two world wars, although in the Blitz of 1941 it was badly damaged by several direct hits, which destroyed large parts of the building and several objects that had been kept there as a so-called 'suicide exhibition'. It has survived financial and political crises, changes in government and funding, and two and a half centuries of wear and tear. The British Museum is as much part of London as St Paul's Cathedral; as much part of British cultural life as the BBC. But what of the future? What are the challenges, opportunities and threats faced by the British Museum as it moves into the twenty-first century?

'When I took over as director,' says Neil MacGregor, 'I was fortunate to inherit a museum that had been physically transformed by my predecessor. We had the Great Court and a lot of extra gallery space created by the departure of the British Library. That was the work of nearly 20 years, when the focus had been on the building itself. Now that's been got right, we can turn our focus elsewhere, and the biggest challenge is how to make the collection usable and able to be enjoyed by the greatest number of people. We have to keep the building and the displays as good as possible; we have to plan our publications and exhibitions in the right order, to appeal to the widest possible audiences. And as much as anything, we're concentrating on expanding the use of the collection outside London, around the UK and around the world. How we can do that safely, and within the limits of our resources, is the question I keep coming back to.'

Getting people through the doors has never been a problem: every year the Museum welcomes nearly 5 million visitors. But as a collection that belongs to the whole of the UK and the world, that is specifically part of London life, is the Museum appealing to all sections of British society? 'We're much more aware now of the different communities in London,' says MacGregor. 'In the last 20 years, London has become ethnically and culturally much more mixed, and we are learning how to use people's understanding of their own cultures to inform our understanding of the Museum's collection and to add to our academic investigation of things. The *Voices of Bengal* season is a perfect example. The fundamental ideal of the British Museum is that it gives universal

access to an understanding of the world, and we are trying to reaffirm that with a new understanding of the complexity of Britishness. You can't now define Britishness without an appreciation of Arab culture or African, Asian, East European or any of the other cultures that make up our population. If we want to understand our society, we must reflect those cultural elements in the way we present the Museum's collection.'

This isn't just noble talk; recent exhibitions at the British Museum have focused on Middle Eastern art and African cultures, the two areas, along with China, that have been identified as the Museum's main focus in the coming years. In the autumn of 2006 a massive sculpture of the Hindu goddess Durga killing the buffalo-headed demon Mahisha was constructed in the Great Court by Bengali craftsmen, prior to display and veneration at the Camden Centre

SONA DATTA

Research Assistant in the
Department of Asia

MY AREA OF SPECIAL INTEREST is the great temple cities of South India – it's what my PhD is on – but I'm also heavily immersed in Bengali culture by virtue of being a Bengali myself. Under the supervision of my senior colleagues Richard Blurton and Brian Durrans, I helped organize the Bengal season. While their experience of the Museum and its collections was invaluable, I was able to contribute my understanding and insight of Bengali language, culture and custom. Exhibitions in other parts of the Museum involved the collaboration with other Bengali groups, such as the Camden Bangladesh Mela Committee and the Tagore Centre. These presentations were complemented by a public programme of over 70 individual events. During the Bengal season many more visitors of South Asian origin visited the Museum than ever before.

    The Museum is constantly developing the way it addresses the communities that make up its audiences. Today, it is much more like a public forum, where different groups can come together to explore their own and each other's cultures. It's really important that people feel they can walk in off the street and 'own' the Museum in some way. They can go into the students' rooms and actually look at the reserve collections, just as they can view the star items in the galleries. I don't think that is widely known.

    A research assistant is like a junior curator, and a large part of my job is inputting information about the collection on to the Merlin database (see page 171). It is a great way to get to know the collection. Many objects have not had their inscriptions properly transcribed or translated, so, where possible, I help out in this area. I have an understanding of Bengali, Tamil and Sanskrit, enabling me to decode and expand the existing information base.

    When the Merlin database goes online, that information will go out into the world for the first time, which is both important and exciting. So people in a village in India, who may never be able to come to London, will be able to access information about our collections for themselves. Online data changes the whole concept of what a museum is: it turns the Museum inside out.

and, finally, ritual immersion in the Thames. It's an exploration of a significant world culture – but it's also a collaboration with the large Bengali community in the London Borough of Camden, in which the British Museum also resides.

    'The project was first suggested to the British Museum several years ago, but it wasn't immediately taken up,' says Sona Datta, a research assistant in the department of Asia. 'However, today the BM is looking at ways of engaging proactively with different communities and making them feel they belong here.

In responding to their interests the Museum has taken a brave and necessary step.' And it worked: during the Durga ensemble's stay in the Great Court, the museum was full of visitors of Indian extraction, many of whom had not been there before. 'It was also very important for them to see me there,' says Datta, 'because I'm Bengali myself, and it shows that we are part of the British Museum too. The Museum isn't just paying lip-service to multiculturalism. It's embracing it wholeheartedly.'

After being exhibited at the Museum, and worshipped at the Camden Centre, the Durga ensemble was taken to the banks of the river Thames at Putney for the last part of its journey. 'We had long and complicated nego-tiations with the Port of London about what we could and could not do with the figures. In traditional Durga worship, or Durga Puja, the figure is completely

Top left: An assistant prepares the clay that will be used to cover the straw structure of the goddess.
Above: The clay is spread on to the surface of the main figure.
Above left: One of the goddess's many hands.
Overleaf: The finished tableau, as high as a London bus, is admired by Sona Datta.

immersed and dismantled. We'd undertaken not to do that; we were going to anchor it to the bank and let the rising tide lustrate [wash over] the figure. But in the event, the community took over. Our neatly organized plan, with clipboards and checklists, went out of the window, and the figure was completely immersed in the water. It really came home to me that this was not just an exhibition or an art project – this was living devotion, just as it happens in South Asia. The Port of London people were fine, they just let the community get on with it. And I must point out that the BM Durga was completely organic and bio-degradable, to comply with the Environment Agency.'

Extending access to the collection takes many forms, both physical and intellectual. In the years leading up to 2010 the entire BM collection will be catalogued in the Merlin database, and when this goes online it will reinterpret the eighteenth-century concept of universal access for the information age. 'Our entire online presence is being redesigned,' says David Saunders, head of Conservation, Documentation and Science. 'Rather than partitioning it off into simple stuff here and complicated stuff there, we'll make it more seamless. You'll be able to find any object, and then it's up to you how deeply you want to explore it. You could just want to identify something you saw casually on a visit to the Museum. You might want to find out the provenance and the history. You might want to go a bit deeper, into more scholarly territory. With the new website, you'll be able to click through to whatever level of information you need.'

To Neil MacGregor, the expansion of the Museum's online presence is the strategy for extending access to the Museum in the twenty-first century. 'All the language of the eighteenth century, about giving universal access to culture, clearly anticipates the arrival of the internet,' he says. 'We have to find a way of making our material usable and possessable by the world, and that's exactly what the website can do. We know that it's massively used outside the UK, so

BRONZE FIGURE OF NATARAJA

I think the bronze figure of Shiva as Nataraja is one of the most beautiful objects in the Museum. Shiva dances upon the dwarf of ignorance, his edict being to know oneself. Shiva's awe-inspiring dance expresses his boundless energy, as he creates, sustains and destroys the cosmos. This single image encompasses all aspects of life – creation, destruction, birth, death, reincarnation, time, fire and water. It's a perfect example of poise and balance – this is South Indian art at its best. You can tell people are fascinated by it from the way they look at it. It is completely hypnotizing.

SONA DATTA, *Research Assistant in the Department of Asia*

'TIGERS CROSSING A RIVER'

This is a painted screen by Maruyama Ôkyo, one of the most important Japanese artists of the eighteenth century, and his pupils. We have quite a lot of works from the school that he founded, but nothing of this stature by Ôkyo himself, until we acquired this. We've just bought it from a dealer, with a very generous grant from the Art Fund, and it's now the star exhibit of the new Japanese Gallery displays.

The subject matter is based on an ancient Chinese legend of a mother tiger ferrying her three cubs across a mountain torrent. One of the cubs is very naughty and has to be kept away from the other two in order to avoid a fight. The painting shows one of the cubs already across the river, licking its fur dry, another cub being carried in its mother's mouth by the scruff of its neck, and the third one, the naughty one, on the far bank, snarling at the water. It's a kind of puzzle piece, about how she's going to get all three to safety.

Ôkyo reintroduced the idea of painting from life into Japanese art, which had become very stylized and stiff by the eighteenth century, and he particularly prided himself on his painting of fur. But it's highly unlikely that he would ever have seen a real, live tiger, so he probably worked from imported Chinese paintings, possibly from looking at a tiger-skin rug, and certainly from watching cats, as you can see. It's impossible to look at the screen without humanizing the animals, and I can't help thinking of a single mum trying to cope with three naughty children.

TIMOTHY CLARK, *Head of the Japanese Section*

we have to develop strategies of making that really useful to the people who need it. One of the most exciting things that's happened recently is a request from the Birzeit University in Ramallah for an online version of our *Word into Art* exhibition about Middle Eastern calligraphic art. Those students obviously can't travel to the UK to see it, and they can't easily travel in the Middle East, but we can create a virtual space where everyone in the Middle East, including Israel, can come together to get an overview of the situation through a study of art and culture. We try to use the collection to create a neutral ground on which potentially hostile people can meet – and the web is the logical extension of that.'

There are also changes afoot in house. Existing galleries are always being reviewed and, when necessary, redesigned. 'Sometimes we need to rethink the way that objects from the permanent collection are displayed,' says Xerxes Mazda, head of Learning and Audience. 'In the past, one of the approaches has been to put all objects of a particular kind in a case, so you have a lot of pots, for instance, in one case and a lot of prints in another. That isn't always the most engaging way of doing things. What we're trying to look at more is telling stories about cultures, exploring themes and, increasingly, asking questions rather than presenting facts. At the moment, we're redesigning the Japan Gallery, and we've worked closely with the curator to decide key themes and storylines. So, for instance, we'll have a whole section on samurai, juxtaposing swords, scrolls, ceramics and so on. It's about mixing materials to get a deeper understanding. You can still go into the gallery and just look at stunning objects if that's what you want to do – but if you're really interested in the history of a culture, you can spend an hour or so in that gallery and follow the social history of Japan.'

The British Museum has always worked on principles of universal access – and that's a concept now being recognized in legislation as well. The Disability Discrimination Act 1995, revised and extended in 2005, has been a catalyst for museums and other public institutions throughout the UK to look at new ways of serving disabled visitors – and that doesn't just mean stair ramps. 'When we're curating an exhibition or refurbishing a gallery we specifically address how it speaks to deaf and visually impaired people, or people with mobility difficulties,' says Jane Samuels, the Museum's access manager. 'It's not just about physical access; it's about intellectual and sensory access as well. Do we have good audio descriptions for deaf people? Are there braille and handling objects in place for the visually impaired? Are displays at a level that can be comfortably seen by people in wheelchairs? You have to make sure that disabled people get as much out of it as they can, and it would be difficult for them to gain intellectual access to our collection if we didn't provide specific services for their needs.'

> The British Museum has always worked on principles of universal access

The 2006 Michelangelo exhibition was an object lesson in just how far concepts of intellectual access can be taken without compromising the curatorial integrity of an exhibition. 'I came on board at quite an early stage,' says Samuels. 'It's important the audio guide is not just a guide for sighted people but also contains proper audio descriptions of the objects for visually impaired people. For Michelangelo, I also commissioned some tactile drawings – simplified drawings, in raised line, of important pieces, so you can feel the image. We had large-print guides available too – and they actually proved to be very popular with everyone, not just people with sight difficulties.

'There are also broader issues of signage and wheelchair access that were addressed in the Michelangelo exhibition. We worked closely with the design team to make sure that the lecterns were accessible for wheelchair users, and that the angle of the label text was sufficient. If it's horizontal, it's very difficult for wheelchair users to read. Temporary exhibitions are a great way to try out new ideas.'

The Disability Discrimination Act also obliges public institutions to extend their services to people suffering from mental distress, something the British Museum has been doing through a Museum Studies course run in partnership with two Further Education colleges. People on these courses come into the Museum once a month for handling sessions with curators, and to visit exhibitions or galleries, and the results have been impressive. 'If you're recovering from

Right: *Throne of Weapons*, the large sculpture made by the artist Kester out of decommissioned weapons from the civil war in Mozambique. The *Throne* toured the UK in 2005 to highlight issues related to conflict and creativity in Africa and worldwide.

mental distress,' says Samuels, 'one of the biggest issues is rebuilding self-esteem and confidence. Contact with the British Museum's collection, in a safe and nurturing environment, is a great way of reconnecting people to the wider culture and giving them a sense of ownership. Going back into the public sphere can be intimidating, and this helps them feel that they have a right to be there. There is tremendous enthusiasm from the people on these courses. We also find work-experience placements for a number of them, which have proved to be enormously successful and inspiring for the students who participate.'

But what about people who can't get to the Museum at all? Can they reasonably expect any kind of physical access to the collection? It seems so. An innovative access project in 2005 took items from the collection into north London's Pentonville Prison, targeting people who quite clearly couldn't breeze through the doors on a Sunday afternoon. 'A prison is a perfect example of an audience with access issues,' says Samuels. 'There are issues here that are right at the heart of what the Museum is trying to do. Rehabilitation is a key priority in prisons, and offending is often a result of poor educational and economic opportunities, so it's imperative to take our collections into those environments.'

The object chosen for the first pilot project with Pentonville was the *Throne of Weapons*, a large contemporary sculpture made by the Mozambican artist Kester from decommissioned weapons handed in following the end of the Mozambique civil war in 1992. The British Museum acquired the *Throne of Weapons* in 2002, and it's been shown in London and all around the UK in places ranging from schools, community centres and cathedrals to museums and government premises. Reactions have been powerful wherever the piece has been shown, particularly so in Pentonville Prison.

'The *Throne* was placed in the prison chapel, which was a perfect setting for it. It's a very ambiguous piece, and the prisoners responded to that immediately. At first they were horrified: they felt that it glorified violence and was all about the power of the gun. We worked with them and developed a film-making project with some of the prisoners, and gradually they unravelled different layers of meaning and saw that it could also be about peace and reconciliation. They became very involved in this discourse and explored it through debate, art, music and writing; some of the songs and poetry they produced were extraordinarily impressive. They were a talented group of people. Several of them had first-hand experience of using guns, and focusing on the *Throne of Weapons* was a way of talking about their own personal experiences. They were speaking of respect for human life, about the morality of gun use – and those are things they don't often debate or analyse.'

The challenge of extending access to its collections is something that the British Museum addresses internally, with initiatives in the London base, around the UK and around the world, with touring exhibitions and loans. But what about those challenges that come from outside? How does the British Museum negotiate an ever-changing, often dangerous international situation that strikes at the very heart of its work?

'My world changed completely in 2003,' says John Curtis, Keeper of the department of the Middle East, which includes, among other flashpoints, Iraq. 'Up until then, we were managing to maintain relations with museums in Iraq, to keep our work going in the Middle East. But since the Allied invasion of Iraq in 2003, things have got very bad.'

In April 2003, at the height of the Iraq War, the National Museum of Iraq in Baghdad was evacuated and subsequently looted by Iraqi insurgents. Some 40 iconic and priceless pieces were stolen from the public galleries, while many thousands of smaller pieces were removed from the storage rooms. The US government was criticized for doing nothing to protect the museum after the occupation of Baghdad, and in April 2003 Curtis went out to the city to report on the situation, followed by a longer visit with a team from the British Museum in June 2003. BM curator Sarah Collins was also attached to the Coalition Provisional Authority for three months.

Right: Damage to the National Museum of Iraq in Baghdad, April 2003.

THE DEPARTMENT OF THE ANCIENT NEAR EAST covered all the cultures of the Middle East from prehistoric times up to the beginning of Islam in the seventh century AD, from the Mediterranean coast to the Iranian border, from Saudi Arabia up to the Caucasus, plus a bit of the western Mediterranean, where there were Phoenician colonies. And we've recently brought in the Islamic and modern Middle Eastern collections and their curators because it seems to make more sense to have all the material together. So we are now the department of the Middle East. The languages we use are the same, the important books are often the same, and we share sites that have had uninterrupted occupation from ancient times right through the Islamic period. The term 'Middle East' can seem rather loaded, of course; you automatically think of political hotspots, terrorism and so on. And it's true that the region does contain Iraq, Iran, Lebanon, Israel and the Palestinian Autonomous Authority. But seeing as we deal with problems resulting from the instability in that region all the time, it's not inappropriate.

JOHN CURTIS

Keeper of the Department of the Middle East

I studied history followed by Middle Eastern archaeology, then I spent two years in Baghdad writing my PhD – I had a fellowship at the British School of Archaeology in Iraq. I was appointed as a research assistant at the British Museum in 1971, and I've been keeper of the Middle East department since 1989. There was a period of relative stability in the area when I was first here, up until the Iranian revolution in 1979, which overthrew the Shah and established the Islamic Republic and the rule of Ayatollah Khomeini. Things have been quite rocky since then, but even during the Iran–Iraq War of 1980–88 it was possible to go to both countries. It's only since the invasion of Iraq in 2003 that things have been very difficult, at least in Iraq.

The British Museum has an important role to play in this situation. Ten years ago, we might not have responded to events on the international scene, but Neil MacGregor has a good understanding of our role as cultural diplomats, how we must get involved with what's happening and explain it to the public. The collections that we have in this building are related to current events all around the world, and it's only by looking into the past that you can ever hope to understand the present or plan for the future. Sometimes people criticize the BM for getting involved in 'politics', but it's an intrinsic part of what we are. We can't just show this material as dead objects. If it's going to stay alive and meaningful, we must relate it to what's happening in the world today.

Our job is not to comment on the political rights and wrongs of the situation. We can only speak up for the cultural heritage, to say when it's being damaged or lost, and to do whatever we can to remedy that situation, and to interpret its significance in the present. We have strong cultural links with Iraq – we're one of the few British institutions that does – and I think that transcends any political position. We have to speak up for the museums and historical sites in Iraq because nobody else will. And one of the most important messages we can give is that we must never be complacent; we must never take our cultural heritage for granted. If that kind of looting and destruction can happen in Baghdad, it can happen anywhere. Order can break down into chaos – look at New Orleans after hurricane Katrina in 2005 – and someone has to protect the world's art and culture. It could happen anywhere.

THE DYING LION

This stone panel is from the north palace of Ashurbanipal at Nineveh, and it's probably the finest Assyrian sculpture to have survived, even though it's quite small compared to some. There's a degree of naturalism that you hardly ever find in Assyrian reliefs – the lion is shown squatting on its haunches, struck by an arrow, dying but struggling to remain upright. I think the artist is expressing some sympathy with his subject.

I 'rediscovered' this piece; it was thought to be lost for a long time, even though it was very well known and appeared in the illustrations of all the books on the subject. Nobody knew where it was; it had disappeared around 1850. In 1992, out of the blue, I got a letter from a lady in Hampshire who had in her possession an Assyrian relief, and she enclosed a photocopy of a book illustration with an arrow pointing to the 'Dying Lion' saying, 'This one'. At first I thought it must be a cast, but I was sufficiently interested to drive down and take a look. And there it was, in a lovely, Victorian wooden frame, hanging on her wall. This lady, Lilian Boutcher, was the granddaughter of one of the people who worked on the BM excavation where it was found, and it had been passed down in her family. And she handed it over to us!

JOHN CURTIS, *Keeper of the Department of the Middle East*

'I had very good relations with the Iraqi Department of Antiquities,' says Curtis, 'because I'd been going there every year, even after the first Gulf War in 1990. So when the museum was looted, I tried to contact its director, Donny George. He'd been trying to call me, but the phone lines were down – so eventually we managed to make contact through the *Channel 4 News* diplomatic correspondent, Lindsey Hilsum, who had a satellite phone. I went out to Baghdad as soon as I could – I was the first archaeologist to arrive in the city after the looting. The damage was awful. So many things had been stolen, really priceless things that belong to the whole of humanity. And there was terrible damage to the building as well. As the museum was an official building, the looters associated it with Saddam Hussein and just wanted to destroy as much as they could. They turned over bookshelves, destroyed files, smashed things in every room. It was a convenient target on which to vent their anger, and nothing was done to stop them.' At the time of writing, over 8000 objects are still missing from the museum.

Following that initial visit, Curtis returned to London with Donny George for a press conference that told the world the extent of the looting. 'We drew up lists of missing objects, and we went back again in the summer of that year to draw up an emergency plan of conservation work. But it hasn't been possible to carry out any of that because the security situation is getting worse and worse. We were going to bring international teams into Baghdad and to the major archaeological sites, but that just hasn't happened.'

It wasn't just in the Baghdad museum that things had been damaged, as Curtis testified when he was asked by the Iraqi Ministry of Culture to go to Babylon to report on the damage caused through its having been turned into a military camp. 'The damage was dramatic. About 300,000 square metres of the site had been covered with compacted gravel and treated with chemicals, which will actually contaminate the archaeological deposits for all time to come. There were "fuel farms" on top of the gravel – basically tanks of diesel fuel, where they filled up their vehicles – and there's a lot of leakage. They'd dug huge trenches, nearly 200 metres long, straight through archaeological deposits. And just having all those troops on the site caused a lot of damage. My report showed that the coalition as a whole had treated the Iraqi cultural heritage in a very cavalier way. Nothing was done to protect the museum or the archaeological sites. I try to be careful to restrict what I say and do to cultural-heritage issues. I'm an archaeologist; I work for the British Museum; my role is not political. My job is to bring to the attention of the public the damage that's being done to that cultural heritage, which doesn't just belong to Iraq, it belongs to the world. It's the history of humanity, and it's being destroyed.'

It's the history of humanity, and it's being destroyed

While relations with the Middle East remain complex and troubled, the Museum is taking an active role in exploring the relationship between East and West through exhibitions and events at home. A season entitled *Middle East Now* in 2006 celebrated aspects of the culture through talks, screenings and debates, all focused around a major exhibition of modern Middle Eastern art. 'One of the main aims of the *Word into Art* exhibition was to remind everybody that in the last 20 years London has become one of the cultural capitals of the Middle East,' says Neil MacGregor. 'For all sorts of reasons, many of them unhappy, London is now a place where Arab culture is being created, almost as though it were itself part of the Middle East. Artists from that part of the world can show their work in London because, tragically, they often can't work and show in their countries of origin. This show wasn't just a way of finding out about Iraq and Palestine and Iran and Israel and so on. It was also a way of exploring the Middle Eastern world of the Edgware Road.'

Word into Art comprised mostly items from the British Museum's contemporary Middle Eastern collection, enhanced by loans, and focused on Arabic traditions of calligraphy and how artists use the Arabic script in their work in both figurative and non-figurative art. As well as works on paper, there were sculptures, paintings on wood and board, and mixed-media pieces incorporating a wide range of materials from clay to gauze. 'It grew out of an exhibition I did a few years ago in Australia, at the Ian Potter Museum of Art in Melbourne, called *Mightier than the Sword*,' says exhibition curator Venetia Porter. 'It was quite a small selection of pieces, drawn largely from the pre-modern collection

KUN CALLIGRAPHIC PAINTINGS BY NASSAR MANSOUR

These, for me, were the most striking pieces in the Word into Art *exhibition. They were two versions done at different times showing the single word* kun, *which means 'be' in Arabic. It is part of the phrase 'Be and it will be', which appears in a number of different chapters of the Qur'an. These allude to the creation of the world and humankind, as well as, specifically, the birth of Jesus. It's a modern piece, but it completely follows the tradition of Arabic calligraphy and is written in the most ancient of scripts, Kufic.*

    I studied calligraphy for a few months with Nassar Mansour, a Jordanian artist, a very serious and exacting teacher. I was only able to study erratically, but it gave me an enormous admiration for these artists and the traditions in which they work.

VIKRAM SETH, *Trustee of the British Museum*

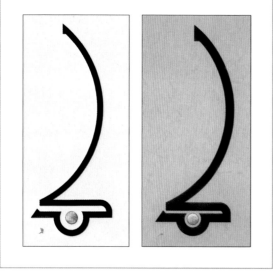

and focusing on the use of inscriptions in Islamic art – but suddenly it was attracting a lot of attention. This was in 2003, just as the Iraq War started, and we had pieces that had been made in Iraq. Place names such as Basra weren't just of academic interest any more; we had a lot of journalists coming. It was my first experience of how you can use the collection in a very contemporary way. The exhibition went on to the Islamic Arts Museum Malaysia in Kuala Lumpur.'

    Venetia Porter's interest in the power of Arabic inscriptions and calligraphy led her to propose an exhibition back at home that would draw more on the modern Middle Eastern collection that she'd been building up over more than a decade. 'The idea was to do a small exhibition at the British Museum, but then I had a lucky meeting with Saeb Eigner, our special adviser on the Middle East season, who proposed something much bigger and introduced the Museum to our partners, Dubai Holding. Once we had support, we were able to look at filling a much bigger space and bringing in a few loans and new acquisitions to make it a more significant exhibition.'

    Thus, with the help of Dubai Holding, *Word into Art* went into the large exhibition space adjacent to the top of the Reading Room, with some large sculptural pieces spilling out on to the stairs and into the Great Court. The interpretation and design team moved in to make the exhibition as accessible as possible to a wide range of audiences, placing Arabic script on the wall, mapping out a storyline that arranged the work thematically, and publishing material that explained the traditions of Arabic calligraphy. Part of the audio guide was voiced by author, calligrapher and British Museum trustee Vikram Seth.

    'Visitors to the exhibition came from across the whole spectrum of the British Museum audience,' says Porter. 'We had the general Museum visitors who are interested in seeing some new art and getting an insight into cultures

WHEN I WAS FIRST ASKED TO BECOME A TRUSTEE of the British Museum, I was very surprised. I'm a writer, and I don't have any particular expertise in archaeology or art history, or in the financial side of things. My first reaction was that it was a great honour, but I didn't think I could take it on. But I'm a great admirer of what Neil MacGregor is doing – he's made the Museum a much livelier, less stodgy place than it used to be – and there's no point in me grouching about the cultural life of this country unless I'm prepared to get involved myself. My family and friends were very much in favour of the idea because they said I was in danger of becoming a recluse unless I did something to pull myself out of my hermit-like existence as a writer. So I thought I'd give it a try.

My interest in the British Museum is twofold. There's the guardianship of the objects in its collection, and there's the challenge of offering them to a wider audience all around the world. Given the contents of the Museum and the provenance of those holdings, it's essential that we should take them to the widest possible audience, both at home and abroad. In 1753 the British Museum was set up for 'studious and curious people' – there was no mention of their nationality. I think that was very far-seeing. It's always attracted visitors from abroad, and now it's able to take its collection to other audiences. I see it not just as the British Museum, but the British International Museum.

I wasn't a great museum-goer before I joined the board. Being tactful, my fellow trustees say, 'Ah, that proves that you represent a different constituency,' which is very kind of them. Now I'm getting more and more interested. I popped into the Jade Gallery the other day, as I had ten minutes to kill, and I lost track of time. I was there for two or three hours, and I missed several appointments.

The board meets four times a year – it's not too arduous, which is important to me because if I'm in the middle of writing a book or travelling around promoting it, I can't give much of my time. We meet in the Hartwell Room, which is a nice high-ceilinged room that gives on to the Museum forecourt. It's quite noisy if you have the windows open, but terribly hot if you don't, so we just have to open the windows and speak loudly. It's nice to hear people in the forecourt, especially the young people running around and enjoying themselves. To me, it's not just about getting them while they're young and turning them into the museum-goers of the future. It's about giving them a good time here and now. The Museum should be for everyone, whatever their age or background, and it should above all be a joy to visit.

VIKRAM SETH
Trustee of the
British Museum

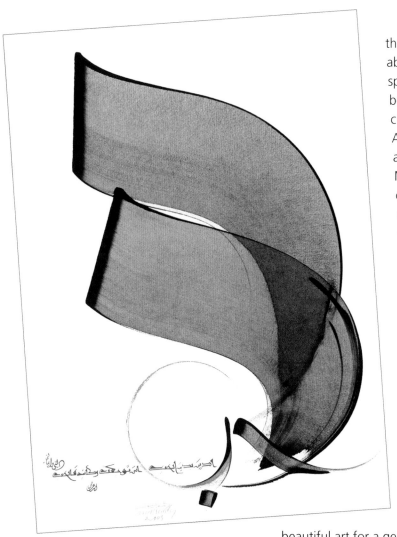

Above: *I follow the religion of love* by Hassan Massoudy, the striking image that was used on the poster for the *Word into Art* exhibition.

that they might not know much about. We had people who were specifically interested in the work because of the light it shed on the current situation in the Middle East. And of course the exhibition attracted a lot of Middle Eastern and Muslim visitors who might not have come to the British Museum before, or who were seeing their own cultures displayed much more powerfully than before. The Muslim children were particularly interesting. At first they'd look at these amazing calligraphic artworks, and they couldn't figure out what they were seeing. Then we pointed out to them that there were letters – here's an *alif* (a), there's a *lam* (l) – and they'd start recognizing words and whole sentences that were familiar from the Qur'an. Their eyes were opened, and they suddenly saw words everywhere. It's possible to appreciate the work just as beautiful art for a general audience, but it also has these specific meanings for people who can read Arabic. The image that we put on the poster, by Hassan Massoudy, is a good example. It's a wonderful double swish of blue, a gorgeous, dynamic design, but it actually represents the word *al-hubb*, which means "love", in Arabic script.'

Audiences flocked to *Word into Art*, reviews were good, and there were articles discussing the calligraphic niceties of different forms of script in tabloid newspapers. 'I was amazed,' says Porter. 'Something I regarded as being of very marginal interest has moved centre stage. People want to know about the cultures of the Middle East, they want to get into the details and understand the complexity of the issues. It all began around 9/11. Up till then there was not much interest in the John Addis Gallery of Islamic art. Then our visitor numbers shot up, and I think it's really interesting that people were coming to the Museum to look at objects from the past as a way of understanding what was happening in the present. We realized that there was a need to make Islamic cultures more accessible, so we redid some sections of the gallery to present the material better. We're saying, "Look, here are some amazing civilizations that we have learnt so much from, they gave us the numbers that we use, a lot of important technology, crafts, beautiful art and literature."'

Word into Art not only presented material celebrating classical trends in Middle Eastern art, but also contained a good deal of work addressing the twenty-first century. The final part of the exhibition, entitled 'Identity, History and Politics', explored the position of women in the Middle East, addressed the destruction of Iraq's cultural heritage and recorded reactions to both Gulf wars. 'There's an urgency to my work in this area that I didn't feel when I first went into the field,' says Porter. 'We're acquiring and showing work that comes from the fulcrum of the modern world, that explores the major faultline in twenty-first-century politics. As a museum, we're at the beginning of a dialogue with the Middle East that will become increasingly important. Arab and Iranian artists are looking to us to take a lead. A lot of people came to see *Word into Art* and said, "We want to do more of this. Can you help us?" Many feel we've put their work on the map; we've opened people's eyes to Middle Eastern art and culture in a way that the artists themselves often cannot do in their own countries. There's an important role for the British Museum in fostering this work in London and the rest of the UK, and then taking it out to the world. If we don't acquire this work, some of it may be destroyed. A lot of contemporary art has been destroyed in Baghdad. We have a duty to get it into the British Museum. This isn't just beautiful work – it's also documentary material for future generations.'

It all began around 9/11. Until then there was not much interest in the gallery of Islamic art. Then our visitor numbers shot up …

Looking to the past to inform the present and inspire the future, the British Museum brings the cultures and the people of the world under one roof in London. At a time when China is re-emerging as a global superpower, the Museum is showing the terracotta army – a perfect opportunity to explore a great culture, forge links between nations and educate a new generation of global citizens. It's the job that the British Museum has done through three centuries – and it's taking that mission boldly and confidently into a fourth.

Overleaf: The British Museum's *First Emperor* exhibition, opening in September 2007, will include a number of the world-famous terracotta warriors from Xi'an, China.

Further reading

The British Museum Press publishes a wide range of titles on the collections of the British Museum and the civilizations they represent. These are a selection:

The British Museum
The British Museum: A History, David M. Wilson (2002)
The British Museum A–Z Companion, Marjorie Caygill (2005)
The Collections of the British Museum, ed. David M. Wilson (3rd edn, 2003)
The Great Court and the British Museum, Robert Anderson (2nd edn, 2005)
Treasures of the British Museum, Marjorie Caygill (2nd edn, 2007)

Africa
Africa: Arts and Cultures, ed. John Mack (2000)
Masterpieces of the British Museum: The Head of an Ife King from Nigeria DVD (2006)
Printed and Dyed Textiles from Africa (Fabric Folios series), John Gillow (2001)
Silk in Africa (Fabric Folios series), Chris Spring and Julie Hudson (2002)

Americas
First Peoples, First Contacts, J. C. H. King (1999)
Masterpieces of the British Museum: The Aztec Double-Headed Serpent DVD (2006)
A New World: England's First View of America, Kim Sloan (2007)
Textiles from Guatemala (Fabric Folios series), Ann Hecht (2001)
Textiles from Mexico (Fabric Folios series), Chloe Sayer (2002)
Turquoise Mosaics from Mexico, C. McEwan, A. Middleton, C. Cartwright and R. Stacey (2006)

Asia
The British Museum Book of Chinese Art, ed. Jessica Rawson (2nd edn, 2007)
Chinese Art in Detail, Carol Michaelson and Jane Portal (2006)
First Masterpiece of Chinese Painting: The Admonitions Scroll, Shane McCausland (2003)
Floating World, John Reeve (2006)
Islamic Art, Barbara Brand (1991)
Japanese Art in Detail, John Reeve (2005)
Korea, Jane Portal and Beth McKillop (2000)
Miao Textiles from China, Gina Corrigan (2001, repr. 2006)

Ancient Egypt
British Museum Book of Ancient Egypt (2nd edn, 2007)
Concise Introduction to Ancient Egypt, T. G. H. James (2005)
How to Read Egyptian Hieroglyphs, Mark Collier and Bill Manley (1998)
Masterpieces of Ancient Egypt, Nigel Strudwick (2006)
Pocket Guide to Ancient Egyptian Hieroglyphs, Richard Parkinson (2003, repr. 2007)
Rosetta Stone (Objects in Focus series), Richard Parkinson (2005)

Ancient Greece and Rome
British Museum Book of Greek and Roman Art, Lucilla Burn (1991)
The Elgin Marbles, B. F. Cook (2nd edn, 1997)
Greek Architecture and Its Sculpture, Ian Jenkins (2006)
Greek Vases, Dyfri Williams (1999)
Hellenistic Art, Lucilla Burn (2004)
The Warren Cup (Objects in Focus series), Dyfri Williams (2006)
The Parthenon Frieze, Ian Jenkins (2002)

Ancient Games
Games: Discover and Play 5 Ancient Games, Irving Finkel (2005)

Britain and Europe
Celtic Art, Ian Stead (2nd edn, 1997)
Enlightenment: Discovering the World in the Eighteenth Century, ed. Kim Sloan (2005)
The Lewis Chessmen (Objects in Focus series), James Robinson (2005)
Masterpieces of the British Museum: The Lewis Chessmen DVD (2006)
Masterpieces of the British Museum: The Sutton Hoo Helmet DVD (2006)
Roman Britain, T. W. Potter (2nd edn, 1997)
The Sutton Hoo Helmet (Objects in Focus series), Sonja Marzinzik (2007)
Treasure: Finding Our Past, Richard Hobbs (2003)

Clocks and Watches
Clocks, David Thompson (2005)

Coins
Money: A History, Catherine Eagleton and Jonathan Williams (2nd edn, 2007)

Conservation and Scientific Research
Earthly Remains: The History and Science of Preserved Human Bodies,
    Andrew T. Chamberlain and Michael Parker Pearson (2004)

India and Pakistan
Embroidery from India and Pakistan (Fabric Folios series), Sheila Paine (2001, repr. 2006)
Hindu Art, T. Richard Blurton (1992)
Indian Art in Detail, Anna Dallapiccola (2007)

Middle East
Ancient Persia, John Curtis (2nd edn, 2000)
Art and Empire: Treasures from Assyria in the British Museum, eds J. E. Curtis
    and J. E. Reade (1995)
Assyrian Sculpture, Julian Reade (2nd edn, 1998)
The Bible in the British Museum: Interpreting the Evidence, T. C. Mitchell (2nd edn, 2004)
Canaanites, Jonathan N. Tubb (2002)
Embroidery from Afghanistan (Fabric Folios series), Sheila Paine (2006)
Embroidery from Palestine (Fabric Folios series), Shelagh Weir (2006)
Forgotten Empire: The World of Ancient Persia, ed. John Curtis and Nigel Tallis (2005)
Islamic Art in Detail, Sheila Canby (2005)
Masterpieces of the British Museum: The Assyrian Lion Hunt Reliefs DVD (2006)
Mesopotamia, Julian Reade (2nd edn, 2000)
The Queen of the Night (Objects in Focus series), Dominique Collon (2005)
Word into Art: Artists of the Modern Middle East, Venetia Porter (2006)

Oceania
Hoa Hakananai'a (Objects in Focus series), Jo Ann Van Tilbury (2004)
Pacific Encounters: Art and Divinity in Polynesia 1760–1860, Steven Hooper (2006)

Prints and Drawings
Looking at Prints, Drawings and Watercolours, Paul Goldman (2nd edn 2006)
Masterpieces of the British Museum: Dürer's Rhinoceros DVD (2006)
Michelangelo Drawings: Closer to the Master, Hugo Chapman (2006)
Prints and Printmaking, Antony Griffiths (1980)

For a complete list of British Museum Press titles, please visit the British Museum Company website at www.britishmuseum.co.uk. For further information about the British Museum and its collections, please visit the British Museum website at www.thebritishmuseum.ac.uk.

Index

Picture credits

BBC Books would like to thank the following individuals and organizations for providing photographs and for permission to reproduce copyright material. While every effort has been made to trace and acknowledge copyright holders, we would like to apologize should there be any errors or omissions.

Page 18 Mary Evans Picture Library; 85 (top left) SWNS.com; 85 (top right) © Ken Allen; 113 (left) Private collection; 124 (top left) Courtesy of the artist and Pace Editions Inc.; 124 (top right) © The Estate of Keith Vaughan/DACS, London 2007; 124 (bottom) © Lucian Freud; 125 © Rob Carter; 126 © DACS, London/VAGA, New York 2007; 131 (top) TopFoto.co.uk; 137 Colin McPherson/Corbis; 143 NI Syndication; 154 © Romuald Hazoumé 2005 (artwork), © Benedict Johnson 2006 (photography); 155 Jason Lee/Reuters/Corbis; 174 © Kester; 176 Patrick Robert/Corbis; 180 (both) © Dr. Nassar Mansour; 181 Camera Press/Leonardo Cendamo/G/N; 182 © ADAGP, Paris and DACS, London 2007; 184–5 akg-images/Laurent Lecat.

Photographs on the following pages © BBC: pp. 14–15, 24, 29, 34, 36, 38, 43, 55, 56, 58, 60, 68, 69, 73, 76, 102, 103, 136, 147, 150, 157, 160, 162 (right), 163, 168, 169 (all) and 170.

Images on the following pages © The Trustees of the British Museum: pp. 10, 13 (both), 19, 21, 28, 40, 45, 46, 50, 51, 52, 53, 62, 63, 64, 65, 67, 70, 71, 72, 77, 78, 80, 82, 85 (bottom), 86, 87, 93 (both), 95 (both), 97, 100, 104, 105, 109, 110, 111, 113 (right), 115, 117 (both), 118, 119, 120 (both), 131 (bottom), 133, 135, 140, 141 (both), 144, 146, 150, 151 (both), 152, 158, 161, 162 (left), 167, 171, 172 and 178.

Photographs on the following pages © Tino Tedaldi: pp. 2, 3, 6, 7–8, 17, 22–3, 26–7, 31, 35, 39, 44, 49, 59 (all), 66, 75, 81, 89, 90, 96, 107, 114, 116, 122, 127, 128, 129, 142, 145, 149, 165, 166 and 177. Photographs on pages 11 and 108 © Cath Harries. Photographs on pages 33, 84, 152 and 164 © Christopher Tinker.

Endpapers: London Aerial Photo Library/Corbis.